# Myakka

## Second Edition

## P.J. Benshoff

Pineapple Press, Inc.
Sarasota, Florida

Inquiries should be addressed to:

Pineapple Press, Inc.
P.O. Box 3889
Sarasota, Florida 34230

www.pineapplepress.com

Library of Congress Cataloging-in-Publication Data

Benshoff, P. J.
   Myakka / P. J. Benshoff. — 2nd ed.
      p. cm.
   Includes index.
   ISBN 978-1-56164-444-5 (pb : alk. paper)
   1.  Myakka River State Park (Fla.)—Guidebooks. 2.  Outdoor recreation—Florida—Myakka River State Park. 3.  Natural history—Florida—Myakka River State Park.  I. Title.
   F317.M92B46 2008
   975.9'61—dc22
                                                    2008040705


Second Edition
10 9 8 7 6 5 4 3 2


Design by Shé Heaton

# Foreword

Among Florida's more than 150 state parks, Myakka River is certainly one of the "crown jewels." Its size, in conjunction with adjacent public lands and private lands with conservation easements, ensures that its ecosystems will be viable as long as land managers are diligent in their stewardship. A diverse array of habitats and many years of freedom from any form of harassment have produced a readily observable animal population, much to the delight of the park's quarter of a million visitors each year.

Most visitors to the park want to know, "Is this the place where you can ride the airboat?" Many are content just to catch a glimpse of an alligator. But the park offers far more to those who elect to partake of the many adventures Paula Benshoff has penned or embark on their own. Clearly, she is enamored with the park and its environs. You will share her joy in viewing a panorama of prairie wildflowers responding to a fire's passing and sense her wonderment at how a land can be parched one month and inundated by seemingly endless rainfall (and its ensuing runoff) the next. Hear the sonorous snoring of gopher frogs, the bellowing of alligators, or the bugling trill of sandhill cranes and you will appreciate how she so lovingly describes the park's many denizens and their habits so that you may find and enjoy them. Each adventure will make you thirst for another.

Having overseen the management of Myakka River State Park for nearly twenty-two years, I have been privileged to be a part of the restoration of an ecosystem that had suffered from what can best be described as benign mismanagement. Early land managers lacked the ecological knowledge we now possess, so actions taken or not taken were often detrimental to flora and fauna. Paula weaves history and science into a vivid tapestry of adventures so you may better understand why things are as they are. It is thanks to Myakka's dedicated staff, such as Paula Benshoff, that you will revel in this wonderful park and better appreciate what was, what is, and what is yet to be.

Robert Dye
Park Manager

# Table of Contents

# *List of Maps* ⚜

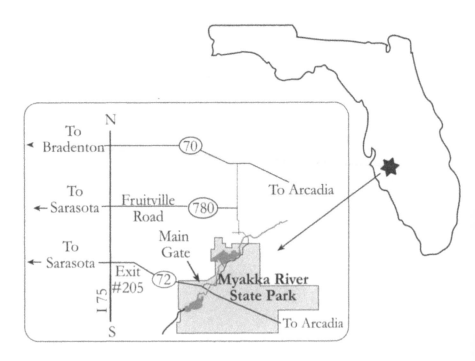

Myakka River State Park SR 72 entrance: North 82°14'21.8   West 82°19'00.2

# ❧ List of Illustrations ❧

# Acknowledgments

No words can express the deep gratitude I have for Robert Dye, who changed my life forever when he took a chance and hired me as a park ranger. He has given me an education no institution could begin to rival, a career with all the elements that one could dream of, and a lifestyle unrivaled by any I could imagine. I appreciate his patience, his inspiration, and his contribution to this book by way of the foreword and editing.

I thank Julie Morris and Pineapple Press for giving me the opportunity to share my appreciation of Myakka with the world. Thank you, Harry McVay, for finding the time to draw upon your many years of experience with Myakka and to illustrate its beauty and diversity so my readers can see it through your eyes and your pen.

Most of all, I thank Jean Huffman, whose patient editing and comments forced me to rewrite each chapter over and over until I got it just right. I relied heavily on her insight into the world of Myakka for she has the ability to perceive its most significant facets though obscured by layers of insignificant rhetoric. And, of course, thank you, Richard, for enduring so many late nights on the computer and so many household tasks left undone.

# 1

# Myakka Magic

*"Jack harnessed the horse and hitched him to the cart. We loaded in our tent, blankets, provisions, ammunition; he took the lines and we were off for a four days' camp hunt on the Myakka River. For several years past I have heard the praises of this mystic region sung by sportsmen who have visited it and experienced its charms."*

G. O. Shields, *Hunting in the Great West*, published 1883

A real estate broker, a teacher, an entrepreneur, and the owner of a soda shop encircled their blazing campfire under a tentacle of the mammoth, sprawling live oak. The gnarled and twisted giant looked as if it had been nourished by the adjacent river since the beginning of time. This camping trip was meant to be the remedy for the stress and fatigue of doing business in a hectic, modern economy. But instead of simply savoring the starlit spring sky so intensified by the late cold snap, the men were fervently engrossed in discussing an issue that had been troubling each of them.

The trip had begun as a hunting expedition, but the four men had failed to discover a single turkey or deer throughout the entire day. It was the teacher who reminded the group how plentiful wildlife had been in the days of his youth, especially here on the old picnic grounds. Why, the Myakka River was world-renowned for its abun-

1

dance of game, but with so many people moving to the area and so many changes occurring . . . Something had to be done or nothing would be left for posterity. It was the real estate broker who came up with an idea. Why not form a sportsmen's club to sponsor wildlife protection laws, similar to what had occurred in his home state of New York? They all agreed to the plan, appointed the teacher as treasurer, and each paid his dollar for a year's dues. The year was 1934.

When the men went home the next day, they began the movement that would become a legacy for generations of Floridians. Soon the Sarasota County Fish and Game Association had attracted a membership of several hundred, which included all the prominent citizens of the day. Success was preordained, for everyone who had either grown up in the region or lived there for very long had magical memories of camping along the Myakka River in the days of his youth. The group appointed Judge Paul Albritton and Arthur Edwards as their spokesmen, and by the end of the year the two had finagled the assignment of a camp of Civilian Conservation Corps workers to the banks of the Myakka River. Soon after, Judge Albritton, Arthur Edwards, and Ivey Taylor drafted the resolution for the creation of one of Florida's first state parks.

But before our story continues, we should consider just what or where Myakka is. If you check out a Florida map, you'll find a river and two lakes in Sarasota County that bear the name, along with a city on State Road (S.R.) 70, a private campground, a state forest, and one of Florida's largest state parks with over thirty-seven thousand acres. Just north of the park is an area called Old Miakka, and environmentalists often refer to the remaining natural lands in the Myakka River watershed as the "Myakka Island."

Myakka isn't a place with definite, perpetual boundaries. It is, instead, the place east of Sarasota where nature, rather than man, still rules. Even as development snips at its periphery, innovative preservation initiatives such as the purchase of conservation easements from private landowners continue to increase the amount of acreage under protection.

Those original pioneer activists are no longer with us, but the spirit that motivated them and their love for the land still thrive, as evinced by the deeds of succeeding generations. In 1985 the Myakka River was designated a Florida Wild and Scenic River, providing protection for the portion within Sarasota County. And when land southeast of the state park was threatened with intense development, citizens of Florida rallied in support with their letters and phone calls. In 1994 the 8,245-acre Myakka Prairie was purchased for permanent preservation.

What's so special about Myakka? Why do young couples choose Myakka for their weddings? Why do families scattered across the country make pilgrimages back for reunions year after year? Why do some choose to spend all eternity here, their ashes discreetly spread along the banks of the river by family or friends? And why is it that "old-timers" sojourn back to see this special place one more time or decide to invest the last leisurely days of their lives here, pursuing activities they always dreamed of having time for?

Though for some people, it's the nostalgia of youthful encounters that draws them to Myakka, for many others it is the discovery of a special place to enjoy activities that give them pleasure. Each has a different perspective on Myakka. The fisherman sees the shallow, prolific lakes and twisting river as an angler's challenge. The naturalist perceives a vast, unbroken wilderness where one can still study floral and faunal interactions and observe natural processes at work. The historian studies the architecture and workmanship of the log buildings and stonework crafted by the Civilian Conservation Corps, while the sportsman comes to hike, bike, canoe, run, skate, camp, or bird in a vast playground. Here, families build unity, the stressed find solitude and regeneration, and artists discover new inspiration. Each establishes a unique bond with the land.

In the pages of this book, you will discover the story of the land of Myakka. The chapters take you into shady hammocks of twisted oaks and aerial gardens, down the wild and scenic river, and across a variegated canvas of prairies, piney woods, and wetlands. Each tells the story of a unique facet of this wilderness area and takes you into secret places it would take years to discover on your own.

Whether you're visiting the park for the first time or have frequented the area since childhood, the adventures are sure to awaken your primitive instincts to explore the unknown. The possibilities for new and exciting experiences are unending. You can return to the same places at different times of the year and find enough adventures to last a lifetime. You'll never be one of those people who ask, "What's there to do in the park today?"

*We loaded our game and camp equipage into the cart and about one o'clock P.M., reluctantly bade adieu to the enchanting Myakka, with all its charming associations; its great live-oak forests; its dense sea-ash thickets; its everglades; its flaming-hued water birds; its deer, turkeys, and the thousand and one other attractions that render it so dear to a sportsman and a lover of nature.*

*Though I may in future years visit every famous hunting ground on the continent; though all such trips may be eminently successful, I can never hope to experience more genuine pleasure in so short a period of time than I did in this four days on the Myakka River. I shall ever cherish it in my memory as one of the brightest, most romantic and exciting episodes of my whole life.*

　　G. O. Shields, *Hunting in the Great West*, published 1883

# Adventure 1

## A Sure Thing:
## Animals That Won't Run Away

**Florida panther**

A bald eagle perched on a snag, a Florida panther stalking through the forest, and a great horned owl surveying pine needle–littered sand for a tasty meal—animals you are guaranteed to see if you come to Myakka; that is, as long as you take a trip to the Visitor Center. Located across from the Ranger Station off S.R. 72, it's the best place to go to plan your day at Myakka River State Park.

These animals, preserved by taxidermy, are displayed in real-life habitats complete with photographic backdrops that make you feel as if you are looking out a window into one of the park's natural communities. The pine flatwoods and marsh displays depict shy creatures you are less likely to encounter, such as an otter and a rail. Look carefully and you'll discover tiny critters, like frogs and hummingbirds, that are difficult to spot. The displays seem to challenge you to "name that animal!" Don't worry; the answers are all there in the picture keys if you get stumped.

The panoramic painting entitled *Florida Dry Prairie: An Endangered Land* pulls you right into the park's magnificent grasslands. Brochures explain the plight of this globally imperiled community and its intriguing array of inhabitants. The park sells posters of the painting to promote awareness of this unique habitat.

The favorite exhibit of park visitors, judging from the comments in the guest book, is the amphibian display. Push the buttons and out bellow the sounds of some of the park's anuran creatures, or its frogs and toads. Pig frogs grunt, and bullfrogs chant a deep *jerommmmm*. See if you can find a sound you hear from your own front porch.

And whatever you do, don't miss the Myakka Movies. Whether you want an overview of what there is to do in the park or are curious about Florida prairies, all you have to do is push a button and watch the video of your choice. Each of the five movies plays between three and five minutes, and you'll be entertained and inspired with every push of the button. While you're there, pick up one of the park's bird lists. There are little spaces to check off each time you identify a new bird, and the game makes your trip even more enjoyable.

These are just the highlights. There's quite a bit more: snakes and turtles, wading birds and waterfowl. . . . You'll find answers to all your questions and may even discover a whole new set of mysteries to solve in your upcoming Myakka adventures.

# Adventure 2

## Take a Cruise on the *Gator Gal*

**American coots**

"You can always tell the old coots by the way they line up outside of Morrison's Cafeteria," explained boat captain Wally Fox back in the early 1980s. "Just look out there on the lake. See those little black ducks all lined up? That's how you know they're just a bunch of old coots." That was the first bird I learned to identify on the Upper Myakka Lake. And I never forgot that those little, black, ducklike birds with the white beaks are called coots.

Wally and Jim Fox built the *Gator Gal* back in the 1960s. Wally ran the tour boat and his brother, Jim, took care of the tram tours. Then, when the exotic waterweed hydrilla invaded the lake, making travel across the water with an outboard motor nearly impossible, they converted the craft into an airboat. It was certainly a novel idea—an airboat that could hold up to seventy-five people—and it caught on fast. Before long, Wally was making three trips a day on what he boasted was the "world's largest airboat."

Wally is no longer with us but his legacy lives on. The boat became so popular that the current owners have built another one just like it, only a little bit bigger. Now the *Myakka Maiden* is billed to be the largest airboat in the world. And no one has shown up in all these years to dispute the claim. It draws more people than nearly any other attraction in the area, and instead of one Myakka boat captain, now there are five.

During the busiest time of the year (January through Easter) there can be as many as ten trips a day, and there are days that the tours sell out by noon. As visitors check in at the boat basin (about three miles from the park entrance), they are given boarding passes for one of the tours. When all the boarding passes are distributed, the tours are full for the day. So, during peak season and on busy holidays, be sure to arrive early.

The boat slowly makes its way around Upper Myakka Lake for about an hour, stopping for a closer look at groups of wading birds or a large alligator. Each boat captain has his own special way of interpreting the Myakka story, and repeat visitors to the park have their favorite guides. All the boat captains provide a good bit of gator lore. The best time to see alligators is when the temperature is between sixty-five and eighty-five degrees and the water's surface is calm. They are also more plentiful when the water level is low (usually late winter and early spring).

Wading birds and ducks are also most prevalent when the water level is low. Migrating ducks begin arriving by late October but are not in great abundance until lake levels drop. Feeding opportunities are best for the birds when the water is shallow, exposing the lakeshore. Since eagles and ospreys nest in the park in winter and early spring, that is the best time to see them fishing the lake to feed their hungry offspring.

Park visitors often record their reactions to the tours in the guest log at the Visitor Center. Judging from their comments, each of the captains is quite an entertaining guide.

# Adventure 3

# A Tram Safari

You will want to pack an extra bundle of youthful imagination to reap the full benefits of this adventure. As the string of boxcars pulls away from the boat basin, the tour guide asks the audience to imagine they are no longer modern-day visitors to a state park but are instead Florida pioneers who are heading into the wilds of Myakka to consider homesteading. As you turn off the paved Park Drive onto the backcountry roads, you slowly discover what life in old Florida was like through the eyes of its early settlers.

The tour is a mix of Florida history, folklore, and wildlife observation. The success of the fantasy depends on who is driving the tram that day. One of the tram operators was so genuine in his delivery that people who took the tour would have sworn he had actually participated in the turn-of-the-century stories he told.

The route will take you over the old Seaboard Coastline Railroad, up an old road built by the Civilian Conservation Corps, and back out Ranch House Road to Park Drive. Though you are not likely to see many animals in the middle of the day, you will learn to detect clues of the presence of wildlife as you pass through shady hammocks, pine flatwoods, fertile marshes, and sunny prairies. The trip lasts about an hour.

Myakka Wildlife Tours' Tram Safari runs only from December 16 through May 31. The posted schedule lists two tours a day but during the height of the season there may be up to four tours daily. Advertisements urge visitors to arrive early in order to obtain seating. During peak season (January–March) and holidays, tickets may sell out hours in advance of a tour.

Whichever tour you choose—tram or airboat—you'll be offered a half-price discount on the other tour. Just save your ticket and either use it that day or come back another time. Each time you come to the park to take the tours, you will be charged the normal entrance fee at the gate. Tickets are sold on the tram prior to departure. Reservations are not available, but when it is very busy, boarding passes are distributed as is done for the airboat tours.

# Adventure 4

## Beginning with Birding

Whether you're an avid hiker or wheelchair-bound, a scholar or a child, rich or poor, young or old, weak or strong, you can enjoy birding. With such universal appeal, it's hard to imagine a more versatile sport. And what better way to spend a day at Myakka!

A glance at the park's bird list and a short ride down Park Drive reveal the reasons the sport is so popular here: the visibility and variety of bird life. Wading birds strut along the water's edge, unconcerned by gawking spectators; grassy marshes and shallow lakes are seasonally animated with colorful migrating ducks and impetuous shorebirds; and picnic area treetops emit a barrage of tweets, whistles, and chatters. It seldom takes park visitors long to begin wondering what bird they are hearing or seeing.

The most important tool you will need is a good field guide. You can pick one up at a bookstore or the park concession for around $20. (Locals can even check one out of the library without investing a dime in this new pastime.)

What do you look for when choosing a field guide? First, check the date the book was published. Sometimes the World Ornithological Society changes the names of birds; range maps periodically need updating; and recent exotic bird introductions are occasionally added to reflect the variety of birds you may encounter. Next, the most important feature I look for is the book's layout. Guides that offer a photo or illustration of each bird, a text description, and a range map on a two-page spread are most convenient. I don't want to have to turn to the back of the book to see if the bird I am trying to identify frequents Florida.

There are a few other attributes you may find valuable. An arrow pointing out the particular trait that distinguishes the bird from other similar species is helpful. Books may offer special feature pages, such as a hawk or warbler page to help you compare hawks in flight or all warblers with or without wing bars. Books that display a small group of shorebirds, gulls, or other similar-looking birds on a page are preferable to those that display only a single bird on a page.

Some guides use drawings; others have photographs. Most new birders find photographs easier to comprehend, but photo guides often show birds in situations very different from the conditions users are observing. I believe illustrations are the most reliable depiction of birds. Though I keep a field guide or two of photographs on my bookshelf for that mysterious bird I can't seem to identify, I usually take a book of illustrations to the field. Your eye quickly learns to compare the depictions on the page to the live bird in the field.

Binoculars are not a requirement, but they do make it easier to identify birds. If you're not familiar with the various features available in binoculars, don't make a purchase without first doing some research. You'll find plenty of information about binoculars on the Internet and at your library. Park rangers can also provide helpful information about choosing and using binoculars at Beginning Birding classes offered Thanksgiving through Easter at the park. Once you purchase a pair, take time to read the directions. I don't think I have ever given a birding class during which someone didn't say something like, "I never realized there was more to using binoculars than putting them up to my eyes! Wow, what a difference when you know how to use them!"

Good birders learn to use all the clues available to them—beyond color and size—when trying to identify a bird. When I first learned to bird there was a ranger at Myakka who always preached the seven Ss of birding: size, shade of color, shape, silhouette (posture), song, sweep (flight pattern), and site (habitat). Experienced birders develop the ability to perceive such subtle differences in appearance and behavior that they can identify birds novices see only as a speck on a wire or a movement in the marshgrass.

As you enhance your observation skills you begin to notice that a mourning dove always sits in a peculiar posture on electric wires, and that woodpeckers fly with an unusual pattern of alternating wing flaps and dips in the air. You will see that vultures hold their wings in the shape of a V while hawks keep their wings straight as a board. Anhingas fly so high above the earth you can't detect their color, but you can always see how they resemble a stiff arrow that flaps a few times and then glides. Green herons like to sit on a low limb just above the water, watching for fish; great blue herons wade into water and stand still, like a stick, waiting for a fish to swim by. Does the bird fly with outstretched neck or crooked neck? Does it feed on the shore or wade into the water? Does it feed by day or by night? Does it nest in a live pine or a dead pine? Does it fly to the treetops or hide in the shrubs when alarmed? Does it bob up and down or wag its tail? There is a helpful display in the Visitor Center that explains the feeding behaviors of the wading birds.

Where's the best place to bird? It depends on your experience, the time of year, and what birds you seek. Beginners do best with the wading birds. You can see them year-round. They are large and easy to focus on with a new pair of binoculars, and they tend to remain in the same spot long enough to find them in a field guide. Try the large picnic area along the river, just north of the S.R. 72 park entrance. The park bridge (about a mile north of the main entrance) and the picnic area north of the park bridge (Fisherman's Area) are also good spots. Walk west on Powerline Road to the river. Go down to the lake area and walk back to the weir. Drive up North Drive and walk out onto the birdwalk, or bird from your car along the lakeshore on North Drive.

To find particular birds, read up on their natural history first. You won't find a Bachman's sparrow, burrowing owl, or caracara along Park Drive; you have to go out to the prairie. You're unlikely to discover a secluded eagle's nest, but you know eagles will be fishing the Upper and Lower Myakka Lakes to feed their hungry young in winter. Migrating warblers, hawks, shorebirds, and ducks are here in winter and early spring; mottled ducks (Florida ducks) are here year-round.

You can see why birding never becomes boring, even if you've been birding for fifty years. There is always so much more to discover, and there are always new birds to check off your bird list. I can't imagine a better place to begin your life list than at Myakka with a Myakka bird checklist.

# Adventure 5

## Birdwalk Sunset

**Great egret**

Sunset at the birdwalk is a treat any day of the year. But when showers are scarce and marshes dry up, the exposed lakeshore grows exponentially day by day and the birdwalk becomes a frenzied melodrama.

Of course, you can visit this boardwalk that protrudes out onto Upper Myakka Lake anytime. Wading birds and waterfowl feed throughout the day and are as likely to be seen midmorning as when the sun sinks toward the horizon. During the winter/spring season, a park volunteer sometimes sets up a spotting scope in the morning to assist visitors with zooming in on and identifying the myriad feathered creatures attracted to the shallow lake. But at sunset there is a tranquil yet exhilarating ambience that seems to clarify your perspective on life.

As you first walk out onto the wooden walkway, you feel a sense of peaceful quiet. The quiet melts into an amazing cacophony of sounds as your ears tune to unfamiliar tones. It is as if you have walked in on a crowd of people conversing in foreign tongues, until your ears begin to distinguish individual sounds, translating noise into birdcalls and birdcalls into a kind of symphony. There's the low, raucous call of the great blues; the descending-staccato hyena laugh from a group of coots; and a high-pitched, drawn-out *honk-honk* that can only be coming from the moorhens. The sound reminds me of those old dolls that say "Maaaa-maaa" when you turn them over. And there are so many more sounds: a *honk* like a clown horn; the evil, sinister laugh of a villain; soap-opera sobs; scattered *toot-toots*; and then, the rustling throb of wing beats that means a vulture is passing overhead.

A broad, green veldt stretches out from the walkway over a hundred feet or more to the waterline. The green is scarred with small patches of rooted-up black mud where some feral hog has fed a previous evening. When you see the lakeshore like this, it's hard to imagine the birdwalk surrounded by dark water. When summer rains arrive, this mat of green will be inundated by tea-brown water and floating waterlilies. The water may rise so high as to cover parts of the boardwalk.

Out on the water, snowy egrets frolic and dance together as sandhill cranes bow and curtsy, dip and wave, and then pogo-stick back and forth towards each other. A wood stork flies by with wing tips nearly dipping into the water, neck outstretched, beak pointed as if to target his destination. You find yourself holding your breath in anticipation of his landing as he slowly wings on across to the distant shore.

Small clusters of birds fly off on an invisible cue, each species with its own internal clock. The high-pitched chatter of the black-bellied whistling ducks is unmistakable, especially accompanied by the visual flash of white on black. They seem to be irritably complaining to each other as they fly by. Skinny, clownlike black-necked stilts perform antics close to the shore as two crows strut, side by side, at the water's edge, stepping in unison. Your eyes focus on a group of white birds in the distance. With a flap of their wings, they surprise you with a flash of shocking pink. Roseate spoonbills. My companion is intent upon his inventory through a pair of binoculars: "Okay, that makes forty-two pigs, twenty-seven sandhills, and twenty-five . . . twenty-six . . . twenty-seven roseates. Oh, and don't forget that mottled duck over there."

In the middle section of the birdwalk, a large display depicts names and photos of the most common wading birds and ducks in the area. Even if you didn't bring a field guide, you can still compare the pictures to the birds you see and identify each one.

You can sit on one of the benches that line the end of the walkway and watch the change of colors in the sky as the sun approaches the horizon. The buttonbush that pokes its head up above the tall grasses casts longer shadows as the sounds of day's end evolve into the sounds of night. A gator roars, grunts of pig frogs intensify, and what sounds like an eerie wail of agony signifies a limpkin is nearby.

No matter how many times you watch this show, it is always surprising how fast the large, fiery ball in the sky sinks behind the string of oaks that lines the horizon. As darkness seeps in, you can just make out the lone night heron just beginning his vigil, the large gator patrolling the shoreline, and a lone deer feeding by the hammock's edge.

Though the park's operating hours are posted as 8:00 A.M. until sunset, gates are never locked precisely at sundown. Park rangers allow plenty of time for visitors to leisurely watch the sun set before making their way to the exit. You can even buy a park pass and get the gate combination so you can stay and watch the stars come out.

## Adventure 6

## Myakka Woods Sense

**Sand cypress**

Moss doesn't always grow on the north side of trees in Florida, and oak leaves don't always look like oak leaves. Even woods-smart transplants to Florida from our more northern latitudes soon discover the challenge of developing an intimacy with the Florida wilds. Here are a few helpful hints for those with a desire to explore Myakka.

Let's start with the weather. Florida weather is fairly predictable if you realize that the rainy season is from June through September. During this time you can expect daily afternoon thundershowers and flooded trails. The rest of the year, rain usually comes with the passage of a cold front, which is followed by cool, dry, fair weather. Clouds provide clues for predicting the weather. Generally, hazy skies and flat or stratified clouds indicate fair weather, while tall, towering clouds with cauliflower-like tops warn of stormy weather.

Florida's terrain is often covered with dense groundcover, especially in areas that have not recently burned. You will usually find vegetation thinner in areas shaded by large trees and along ecotones, areas between two natural communities, such as a marsh and pine flatwoods. When you're exploring wet areas, notice which plants grow in soft, muddy soils and which prefer sandy, hard bottoms. Don't walk through pickerelweed (*Pontederia cordata*) or fire flag (*Thalia geniculata*) unless you don't mind sinking to your knees in muck. Instead, choose wet areas vegetated with sand cypress (*Hypericum fasciculatum*) to ensure yourself a hard, sandy surface.

Always consult a map to determine the location of landmarks and roads before venturing into an unfamiliar area. You should carry a compass too, but if you find yourself momentarily misplaced without one, there are a few ways to orient yourself. You can use the path of the sun to tell directions, but remember that the sun is high in the sky for several hours during the middle of the day in the summer. In winter, it rises in the southeast, arches south of directly overhead at midday, and sets in the southwest. If you note how the angle of the sun compares to your original heading when you go into the woods and keep the season's sun path in mind, you should be able to find your way back unless clouds obscure the sun.

Should you not make it back before the sun sets, you can wait for the moon to rise (hopefully before sunrise) and navigate by the light of the moon. Like the sun, it also rises in the east and sets in the west.

If you're following a trail on which you plan to return, occasionally look back to see how the trail looks from the other direction. Watch for forks in the trail that you may otherwise overlook on your way in but that may present difficult choices on your way out. If you're hopelessly lost and come upon a fence line, the fence is probably running either east to west or north to south and will eventually lead to a road.

Following a riverbank (advice usually offered in other states for finding civilization) is not the best solution here, however. The Myakka is edged with marshes and meanders in a broad floodplain, making it difficult to follow. A similar problem exists with ponds and marshes. You may plan to encircle a pond and return to your original location without realizing that it is not round but peanut-shaped or part of a long chain of marshes. It is easy to end up completely turned around and a long way from your destination.

Finally, for those of us who find ourselves still in the woods when the sun sinks low in the sky, it is helpful to know how to estimate how much daylight is left. Hold your hand out and measure how many hand widths fall between the sun and the horizon. Each hand width represents fifteen minutes. ❧

# 2

# The Wild and Scenic Myakka

*Our daily walk in search of sport was to the Upper Myakka Lake, about a mile distant from the house, through a pine-forest with undergrowth of palmetto and paw-paw. The pools left by the overflow of the lake we found swarming with alligators; in one not fifty yards in diameter I counted thirty-five of these hideous reptiles, ranging from eight to twenty feet in length. It made us first rather nervous, when wading after duck through water and mud up to our waists, to know that the next step might be on the back of an alligator lying buried in the mud, with the probable result of losing one or both legs, but impunity from such accidents quickly made us bolder. On the lake we found some dozen different varieties of duck, though the large flocks were already beginning to migrate to the north; otters were occasionally met swimming through the water-lilies, and large numbers of them are trapped every season on both the Upper Myakka and the Lower or Vanderipe Lake.*

G. O. Shields, *Hunting in the Great West*, published 1883

W hether you're meandering through a shady canopy of ancient, moss-draped live oaks or snaking through the stark and eerie floodplain marshes that abut the Upper and Lower Lakes, the Myakka presents a different scene with every bend in the river. Then, each of those scenes offers an entirely contrasting setting as seasons change and water levels rise and fall.

The Myakka can be so dry that short sections of riverbed transform into a crusty web of hardened, black mud. During these times, you can trudge across the entire Upper Myakka Lake in only knee-deep water. It can be so wet that roads through the park are accessible only by boat and the water level inside the park's log cabins measures waist high.

The Myakka begins its sixty-six-mile journey in a swamp along the northern fringes of Manatee County. Rainfall feeds the seven tributaries that coalesce in Myakka City just north of S.R. 70. From there, the diminutive, blackwater stream winds its way to the Sarasota County line, where it is crossed by the S.R. 780 bridge. It is here that the river picks up the "Wild and Scenic" epithet. The purpose of the Florida Wild and Scenic designation (like its predecessor, the National Wild and Scenic River Program, which originated more than three decades ago) is not only to "recognize rivers that possess outstanding remarkable scenic, recreational, geologic, fish and wildlife, historic, cultural, or other similar values" but also to "provide protection that will sustain these values for future generations." Only the Myakka River has been bestowed with this distinction in Florida.

Just after its arrival in Sarasota County, the river skulks through the back entrance of Myakka River State Park, widening first into Upper Myakka Lake, then to Lower Lake. Though it is for these twelve miles that the river is most famed, the stream doesn't lose any of its wild and scenic qualities for quite some time after leaving the park. It flows into and out of an expansive county park and several large, county- or privately owned tracts of land before it picks up scatterings of waterfront homes and a couple of fish camps. Then there is a brief visit to Charlotte County on its way to Charlotte Harbor, one of Florida's most productive estuaries.

I always find it amusing to read descriptions of the Myakka written by authors who visit the river once and try to describe it for all time. To one writer it is wild and turbulent, carrying a canoe downstream so quickly that only the strongest of paddlers are advised to take the challenge. To another it is slow and lazy, requiring portage over shallow sections. Some describe it as teeming with wildlife, while others find it hauntingly barren. There are alligators at every bend, or the river is disappointing when not a single alligator shows its beady eyes.

The truth about the character of the river is that it is always changing. As is true of most natural things, just when you think you have it all figured out, it surprises you. Typically, the Myakka is high during the summer rainy season. You don't see much wildlife then. As the river floods its banks and the seasonal ponds and marshes fill with water, wading birds, alligators, and mammals are drawn instead to the shallow, ephemeral wetlands scattered through the pinelands and prairies. Migrating birds are absent at this time, and it's too hot for turtles to bask on reclining palms. Any alligators that remain in the river or lakes stay submerged with only eyes and snouts visible.

In late fall the water levels begin to drop. Migrating birds arrive and wetlands dry up, sending animals back to the river. As the depth of the river and lakes diminishes, concentrations of fish attract flocks of wading birds. Nesting eagles and ospreys hunt the river corridor to satisfy their ravenous offspring while the muddy shoreline is exposed to present a smorgasbord of delicacies for ibises, killdeers, yellowlegs, and sandhill cranes. When the temperature drops, bull gators bask on mud banks, displaying their impressively massive physiques, and turtles balance on logs with feet stretched upward.

But typical is not the rule at Myakka. It's often said that there is no such thing as average annual rainfall in Florida. If we get thirty-seven inches of rain one year and eighty-two inches the next, how accurately can a figure that falls between such disparate numbers describe yearly rainfall? One September may log two inches of rain, the next twenty inches. In some years the river never floods out over Park Drive, requiring closure to vehicles; in other years it happens three times in one season. In the winter of 1996, during what is normally the driest half of the year, Park Drive flooded four times. In the summer of 2003, the river gauge reached an all-time high of 20.33 feet above sea level. The only way to travel to the north gate was by boat or canoe.

Though renowned for its beauty and diversity, the Myakka is not the pristine stream G. O. Shields described in the 1800s. When the land was first acquired for a state park in the 1930s, the priorities were to prevent lightning fires from burning, to minimize flooding of the river, and to prevent the lakes from drying up. Squads of men from the Civilian Conservation Corps promptly dug ditches to reduce flooding in the surrounding lands and to decrease "mosquito breeding grounds." They installed firebreak roads and a fire tower and constructed a concrete weir to hold back the waters of the Upper Myakka Lake. In 1940 an earthen levee was added to the south end of the lake.

Though it would take half a century for park managers to comprehend the detriment of fire exclusion, they realized by the early 1960s there was something very wrong with their approach to water control. Without a drawdown, wading birds and ducks abandoned their winter feeding grounds. Aquatic plants could no longer flush out to the Gulf with rising water levels. They just sank to the bottom of the lake and rotted. The lake's sandy bottom turned into muck. Finally, in 1976, as biologists realized the weir was artificially hastening the death of the lake, culverts were installed to allow water to flow through. Today, we are still plugging and filling ditches to help restore more natural water cycles.

Most of these assaults are subtle—never detected by the untrained eye. Park visitors still see the Myakka as a pristine paradise—bass leaping from the lake's surface, eagles soaring overhead, flocks of ibises probing the shoreline, deer grazing at the water's edge just before sunset. Sometimes someone will question the dark, tea-brown water, thinking it's pollution rather than the natural tannic acids leeched from the leaves of trees in the floodplain. Those who have visited the park throughout long decades notice declines in ducks. But these are creatures as dependent on their breeding grounds as on their winter home. For the most part, the Myakka still appears wild. After all, there aren't many rivers left in the state without development along their shorelines. It remains a challenge for those who love the river to keep the Myakka healthy and wild.

The Myakka is unique, with its shallow lakes, vast floodplain marshes, dense alligator population, and abundant wildlife. It's diverse. Over 750 species of plants grow along the river corridor or within the adjoining woodlands, prairies, and wetlands. The river sustains bobcats, deer, otters, foxes, raccoons, and more than a dozen other mammals. Thirty-five kinds of fish, six types of turtles, four salamanders, and over a dozen frogs and toads rely on this aquatic system, while over 150 different birds live along or visit its shorelines.

It seems no matter how well you get to know it, the river continues to inspire awe and reverence each time you paddle it. It always presents new mysteries to solve and unexpected discoveries. A gator's nest, a pair of limpkin chicks, a vulture roost, or a 140-foot-deep sinkhole—each canoe trip or hike along the banks holds a surprise. The Myakka is still wild enough for an adventure but tame enough that a novice paddler can enjoy it.

**Peninsula cooters**

# Adventure 1

## Canoe the Myakka

Though the entire trip could probably be done in a long summer's day, most canoeists wouldn't get much joy out of such a marathon. So I have divided the river into shorter trips that can be leisurely savored rather than bravely endured. Read descriptions of all the segments before you plan your journey, as you'll find valuable tips in each section that are helpful for any of the excursions. Take time to check out a video on canoeing from your local library to avoid being one of those "expert" canoeists who spends the entire trip down a river switching the paddle from one side of the canoe to the other or bouncing between canoe banks. You won't believe the difference a few minutes spent learning the basic strokes will make—for both your river experience and your relationship with your paddling buddy.

### River Gauge

The park's river gauge was installed north of S.R. 72 in the mid-1930s. Apparently someone just put a measure divided into hundredths of a foot on a post next to a picnic area. The gauge readings have been faithfully recorded for over sixty years. But until a few years ago, when a survey permitted resetting the gauge to reflect the actual above-sea-level (ASL) elevation, the readings indicated only how far the water level was above the 0 point on the gauge, which was nailed randomly to the post. The survey determined that you must add 7.92 inches to the original reading to determine the ASL elevation. You can get the ASL reading by calling the park office.

The National Weather Service uses readings that are electronical-

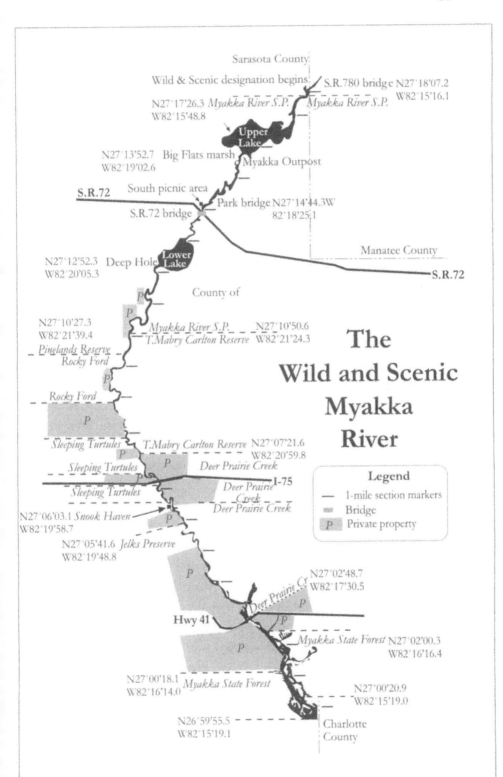

ly transmitted through equipment installed at the gauge site. When TV or radio newscasters refer to gauge readings for the Myakka, they are using the unconverted readings. The park's web page (www.myakkariver.org) links to a site that provides automatically updated gauge readings, but you must add 7.92 inches to the number displayed for the "Myakka near Sarasota" reading in order to convert it to ASL.

## S.R. 780 Bridge to Upper Myakka Lake

**(Note: Don't try this section when the river is below 13 feet ASL.)**

The road shoulder at the S.R. 780 bridge is narrow and the incline down to the river is steep, but there is room to park a small vehicle. Or you can park at the north park entrance and walk the mile back to the river. If you park inside the gate, note that the north gate is open weekends and state holidays from 8:00 A.M. until 5:00 P.M.

Unlike other portions of the river that can easily be navigated up- or downstream, this section is a bit harder to go up since it is navigable only when water levels are moderately high and the river is flowing. You can forgo an arduous return trip by bringing two vehicles and parking one at the birdwalk, a wooden boardwalk jutting out into the lake from a parking lot on North Park Drive, or at the park concession. The walk back along North Drive from the birdwalk to the bridge is about three miles.

I've always considered this section of the river the most "forbidden." My early attempts in the 1980s to canoe it always failed at some never-ending blockage surrounded by a dense, impassable stand of swamp trees. But drastic changes have occurred upstream, altering the amount of water entering the Myakka River. The river is higher for longer periods of time and does not stay dry as long as it did in the past. These changes in hydrology have caused massive tree die-offs in the river's headwaters (Flatford Swamp) and along some sections of the river north of the Upper Lake. In wet years this part of the river is more accessible to paddlers when water levels are high. Still, it is one of the less-traveled portions of the river. The only places I ever see another boat are near the bridge and at the Upper Lake. Though the Myakka passes through the Hidden River subdivision, the only evidence is a couple of docks and a small mowed area that serves as a private park for the residents. The rest of the trip is swamp and marsh, with a bit of oak hammock where there is higher ground.

I'm always surprised to see so many wading birds along this stretch of the river when the water is high, a time usually known for its lack of bird life. An impetuous little green heron, hunched on the branches of a silver-gray oak skeleton, squawks angrily as he takes flight, splaying his top-notch feathers like some sort of gooney bird. A patient great egret sits confidently in the top of a maple as our canoe glides quietly by. Along the length of two bends in the river we identify every type of heron and egret listed in our field guide except the reddish egret. Even the two species of night herons make an appearance.

Less than two hours into the trip, the river suddenly bursts out into the Upper Lake. Yellow waterlilies and water spangle ferns float on the smooth, blue-gray water below us as a dozen turkey vultures glide gracefully above. The shoreline stretches out nearly to North Park Drive, and a hat accidentally dropped onto the lake's surface moseys along toward the river's end. Just to the left, Clay Gully enters the lake.

It's nearly impossible for the first-time visitor to Myakka to conceive of the variety of scenes that are played out on this very spot throughout the seasons of the year. The faint scent of decaying vegetation permeates the quiet stillness of a hot summer day, the only interruption an occasional lazy squawk from a large, clumsy heron. In the winter the lake is alive with sound: the calls of thousands of ducks dabbling in the shallows, the piercing cries of ospreys and eagles overhead, the honky chatter of coots all in a line, and the noisy jubilee of shorebirds celebrating the miles of exposed, muddy lake bottom that encircle the lake.

A few more minutes of paddling will bring you to the birdwalk. If you left a vehicle at the birdwalk drive the last two miles to the concession for an ice cream cone reward. If you left a vehicle at the concession, you will have another half hour to paddle. But that ice cream cone will taste even better.

# Adventure 2

## Concession to South Picnic Area

**Sandhill cranes**

Canoe and kayak rentals at the park concession make this section of the river the most traveled. Fishermen, birders, and canoeists take off from the boat basin, follow the southwest shore of the lake to the weir, portage around or float over the flooded concrete structure (depending on the time of year and water depth), then meander through Big Flats Marsh toward the park bridge, and end at the South Picnic area and Pavillion just north of SR 72. The trip usually takes one to two hours.

The concrete weir that divides the Upper Lake from the river is usually referred to as "the dam" by park visitors. Unlike traditional dams, the weir dips in the center and allows water to spill over the top and flow down the river. When water levels are low, you can walk across the weir as if it were a small bridge. Canoeists must portage around or over the structure and larger boats are confined to the lake. When lake levels are higher, water covers nearly the entire structure, making it invisible except for the two ends. Canoes and shallow-draft boats can simply float over the top. I never considered the weir ominous until a park visitor related to me how her younger brother drowned at that location when they were children.

The weir is usually a great place to observe wildlife and a favorite fishing destination. On my last trip down the river, seven or eight dozen egrets and ibises congregated below a couple of hundred grackles. The grackles noisily chattered and fluttered back and forth across the grasses on either side of the weir. A limpkin, apparently suffering from insomnia, fished lazily beside a great blue heron. As I glided by within two paddle-lengths of the heron, I silently boasted of my stealth when he didn't take flight. The weir is also a good place to look for roseate spoonbills.

There aren't many places left in this state where you can go and get lost. If you're one of those people who believe it's not truly an adventure if there's no possibility of getting lost, you're going to like Big Flats Marsh. Of course, there's no danger of being permanently stranded in the huge, grassy marsh that abuts the Upper Lake, but when the water level is high, it can be somewhat frustrating for an hour or two trying to find the right channel. Often the widest channel winds to a dead end while a less-inviting path continues on downstream. When the water is very high, any channel will take you to your destination. If you plan to paddle and return the same route during high water, be sure to test your strength against the current. Canoeists sometimes paddle easily downstream, not realizing the effort it takes to return (especially paddling against the wind).

Invasion of this marsh by exotic plants makes this my least

favorite part of the river. Big Flats was once a diverse wetland, patched with clusters of bulrush, the golden blooms of marsh marigold, and the pink spikes of smartweed. Maidencane was probably the dominant grass. Now you seldom see anything but paragrass and West Indian marshgrass in this section of the river. Only the native water paspalum is able to compete in a few places with these aggressive exotics. Invasive aquatic weeds are also a problem in the river and lake.

Thousands of dollars are spent each year to control the purple-flowered water hyacinths and seaweedlike hydrilla that plague the river, just to keep the corridor open.

Near the south end of Big Flats, the river passes under the power line. This was once the site of a railroad bridge, and old-timers tell me it was once the best place in the county to get a passel of speckled perch in a couple hours' time. You fishermen might want to try your luck here. Birders may prefer to look for the power poles, which almost always support large osprey nests.

The river evolves into an entirely different scene, with billowy cauliflower clouds rising above heads of cabbage palms lining the banks. White vine milkweed tumbles out over patches of buttonbush every now and then. Around a sharp bend, large pine trees grow nearly to the water's edge. As far back as anyone can remember, this scenic spot with large oaks leaning down over the water has been called Alligator Point. True to its name, this area almost always harbors alligators. One year I discovered a large gator nest and returned often to check for hatchlings. Myakka old-timers tell a story about a man who was herding cattle across the river at this point and was attacked by an alligator. None of them knew his fate, however. Perhaps this is how the area got its name.

Just above the park bridge, the river passes a small picnic area lined with oaks and palms. Rangers call it Fisherman's Area. The choice of channels can be confusing, so be sure to hug the bank of the picnic area to enter a very narrow but deep channel that winds close to the land. All the other choices lead you to a dead end. Recently this little channel was totally blocked with solidly packed, decaying water hyacinths. We tried alternate routes for about an hour, then returned to the channel along the east bank and resorted to digging out the packed vegetation so we could pass through to the park bridge.

After heavy rains, the bridge also can become clogged with exotic vegetation, making it necessary to portage around. Sometimes the water level is so high you have to duck your head in order to make it under the bridge. A researcher studying bats once told me that the underside of this bridge is a great place to find sleeping bats. I always look, but I'm always disappointed to find nothing but mud dauber nests.

After passing the bridge, you reach what I consider the most beautiful portion of this section of the river. The banks seem to invite you to clamor onto them for a short hike or a leisurely picnic. Next you'll pass the Log Picnic Area (named for its log cabin pavilion). This was the location of the first park concession. You can still see the remnants of the old docks. A wooden, docklike structure also protrudes into the river at this point. It houses equipment that measures and transmits river depth to a U.S. Geological Survey office.

Finally, you reach a large pavilion on the river's edge known as the South Picnic Area. This is your last chance to go up to the Ranger Station to obtain a permit before venturing into the Wilderness Preserve. It is here that some choose to take their canoes out of the water and tote them up to the parking lot. If you're not planning to paddle back to the Upper Lake, you'll want to return to the bridge instead, where you left your vehicle (or a bicycle to ride back to the lake area to pick up your vehicle).

# Adventure 3

## South Picnic Area to Deep Hole

**White ibis**

This portion of the river winds through a 7,600-acre chunk of land called the Wilderness Preserve. You will need a permit from the Ranger Station because the area is limited to thirty persons or ten watercraft per day. Putting into the river upstream at either the Log Picnic Area or the park bridge will add a few minutes to your journey but is well worth reducing the distance you have to carry your canoe to reach the water.

If I had to choose the best section of the river for photographing wildlife, this would be it. Gnarly oaks and graceful palms lean out over the river's surface, providing platforms for basking turtles and patient herons. Egrets, grackles, anhingas, and kingfishers crisscross the river in front of your canoe as moorhens skate across the water's surface. A sleepy limpkin emerges near the bow of the boat as if to jump on for a ride.

This is also where the largest gators haunt the shores. It is these "Tarzan gators"—startled monsters splashing into the river as your canoe rounds the bend—that scare our most novice canoeists, for they seem to imitate the crocodiles in those old movies. (As soon as some damsel fell into the river and the muscled hero rushed to her rescue, a passel of hungry reptiles would slither into the water, heading straight for their prey.) As canoeists paddle down the center of the river, alligators sunning on the banks react by seeking the safety of the deepest part of the river—the middle—thus giving the illusion of pursuit.

The best time of day to photograph birds and alligators is early morning, when they seem less wary of strangers. Cool temperatures, though warm enough for basking, bring gators out onto the banks, where they are easier to photograph. But don't approach them closely enough to scare them into the water when the weather is cold. It consumes energy reserves they may not easily be able to afford since they won't be able to feed again until the weather warms up.

Abruptly the scenery shifts again as the Myakka snakes into the expansive marsh that borders Lower Myakka Lake. I find winding through the walls of exotic grasses eerie and unsettling, like being in an open prairie with the vista just barely obscured by some unnatural hedge. I'm always tempted to stand, teetering in the delicately balanced canoe, in order to glimpse the horizon.

As you navigate the hairpin curves, be sure to notice where a canal intersects with the river. You don't want to mistake it for the river when you canoe back upstream. And as you enter the lake, be sure to look back and memorize the entrance to the river. Otherwise you may make a few false starts before finding your way back home.

Since the Lower Myakka is the shallower of the two lakes, it attracts the largest amount of bird life under certain conditions. As water levels drop, feeding opportunities are often better at the Lower

Lake. Eventually, as the Upper Myakka draws down, conditions equalize, but there is usually a time during the winter or spring when ducks, spoonbills, skimmers, stilts, herons, and grackles congregate by the thousands. Both ospreys and eagles nest close by so they are also a frequent sight in the winter.

Deep Hole is a common destination for anyone venturing into the Wilderness Preserve. There are many stories and legends about this mysterious sinkhole, but a camera lowered into its depths in the 1980s proved it not to be bottomless and revealed the rocky sides of a typical sinkhole. When the water is very shallow, the lower half of the lake dries up completely, leaving only Deep Hole wet and populated by a multitude of huge alligators. One old-timer swears that Deep Hole was always separate from the lake back in the early 1920s and that palm trees grew all the way around it. Since no one has a photograph from that time period, I guess we'll never know.

To reach Deep Hole, head towards the steel radio tower at the south end of the lake. A peninsula of land supporting a couple of palm trees juts out into the lake from the western shore and meets with what looks like the remnants of an earthen dam. The lower the water level, the easier it is to spot.

The trip to Deep Hole takes about two hours under good conditions. "Good conditions" means the water level isn't too low; there's not too much wind; there aren't too many water hyacinths; and there's not too much hydrilla. From Deep Hole you may choose to picnic on the lakeshore, venture down the lower river, or return towards the south pavilion. And don't forget to check out of the Wilderness Preserve before sunset at the Ranger Station.

## Adventure 4

# Lower Myakka River

**Green heron**

The river below Deep Hole certainly must be the wildest part of the Wild and Scenic River. You can reach it by continuing downstream from Deep Hole or by coming upstream from Snook Haven. Either route is a lengthy paddle but well worth the effort. (This section is also inaccessible to larger boats most of the year due to the weir above it and the dam below it.)

Every bend and twist of the lower river displays a new photograph to take. Its leaning palms and huge oaks are reminiscent of the short section of river just south of S.R. 72, but there is so much more of it. It gives you the feeling of true wilderness.

Just after the river crosses the south park boundary, it spills over a dam installed many years ago by the adjacent landowner. Be careful. When the water is flowing, you round a bend in the river and come upon it quickly. At high water, the structure can be shockingly ominous if you are taken by surprise. The land on the west is private property; the land on the east is a county park. I would suggest portaging around on the east (left) side.

You may prefer to access the Lower Myakka from the south when the water level is low. Snook Haven, a county park and restaurant at the east end of Venice Avenue, has a boat ramp that can be used by canoeists and kayakers. The park is open seven days a week and the restaurant serves lunch and dinner. If you want a cabin or campsite waiting when you return from your long canoe trip, make a reservation next door at Venice Campground.

Swamp lilies, giant leatherfern, pickerelweed, and cascades of blooming hempvine line the shore upriver from Snook Haven. High banks and a wall of oaks and palms present the illusion that the river is uninhabited for long stretches, though an occasional rooftop pops up here and there. Wildlife is much more sparse than along the upper parts of the river, for the channel is deeper, not as inviting to wading birds.

Short sections of boat docks, mowed lawns, and houses (built before the Wild and Scenic legislation and setback rules for building went into effect) are a sharp contrast to long stretches of native vegetation. A sign posted on one of the docks beseeches "Please watch for manatees." At another, some wishful thinker posted a "Speed Limit 55" sign, either in protest of or in support of the minimum speed/no-wake restriction that is part of the Wild and Scenic River regulations.

The Lower Myakka is also known for its paleontological treasures. Where the palmettos tumble over twelve-foot-high sandy banks, close investigation may reveal hints of prehistoric life. The area has been popular with amateur paleontologists seeking fossils and sharks' teeth for as long as people have been canoeing the Myakka. The best time to look is after the first rain following a prolonged dry period.

# Adventure 5

## Bass Fishing at the Weir

**Largemouth bass**

If you're fishing for bass and don't plan to wade out into the lake to cast your hook, the best place to try your luck is probably the weir where the Myakka River flows out of the Upper Lake. Take the path from the back of the picnic area behind the park concession. Though luck, skill, and current conditions all play a part in determining your success, fishermen have caught bass weighing as much as twelve pounds at this spot.

The choice of bait for most Myakka bass fishermen is artificial worms like red shad, salt and pepper with green tails, and Culprit red worms. The dark tannic color of the water makes dark lures (especially shades of red) most effective. Weedless hooks are also highly recommended due to the amount of exotic vegetation that plagues the river and lakes. Some prefer true-turn hooks; multi-hooks are not recommended. Fly-fishing with surface-floating poppers is also popular.

One favorite method of Myakka fishing is to cast your line to land just short of a group of floating plants, wait for it to settle, then reel it back in very slowly. Another is to cast into small openings between floating vegetation without using a weight, fishing close to the surface.

When is the best time to fish? Each fisherman seems to have a favorite formula. Spring (especially early April when fish are on the beds and low water levels concentrate them into smaller areas) is usually a favorite time. But some fishermen consider it unethical to fish when these conditions become extreme. Others prefer more moderate water levels, and an occasional angler swears that the only time to fish is when the water floods out over Park Drive. Surprisingly, there are two extremely different opinions on the effect of floodwaters on fishing success: either high water levels inundate the lake with terrestrial insects that compete with your bait and make fishing more challenging, or the high water excites a feeding frenzy that creates great fishing opportunities.

The best times of day to catch bass are said to be an hour or two before sunset and an hour before sunrise. When the barometer plunges (just before a storm or the arrival of a cold front) is also considered to be a prime time. But the best way to judge is probably to observe the conditions where you plan to fish. You can count on good luck when the fish are hitting the top of the water (feeding), causing the little baitfish to scatter. If the water is still (with no action), perhaps you should fish someplace else.

Here are some other places in the park to fish from the bank:
- south picnic area north of S.R. 72 (depending on water levels)
- behind the log pavilion, especially at the river gauge
- Myakka River Bridge (about 1 mile north of S.R. 72)
- Fisherman's Area (picnic area north of Myakka River Bridge, west of Park Drive)

- Boat basin area (depending on water levels)
- Clay Gully Bridge, south of the north park entrance
- Clay Gully picnic area
- Deep Hole (in the Wilderness Preserve), when water levels are low

## Fishing Regulations for Myakka Area

A Florida fishing license is required for anyone over fifteen years of age. Florida residents sixty-five years and older can obtain a lifetime fishing permit without charge. You can fish in your county of residence without a license if you fish with a pole and live or natural bait rather than a rod and reel. Upper Lake, Lower Lake, and the river between the lakes are in Sarasota County. Clay Gully picnic area is in Manatee County.

These are the limits for the Myakka area:

- five black bass (largemouth); all must be at least fourteen inches long; only one may be twenty-two inches or longer
- fifty panfish individually or in total including bluegill, redear sunfish (shellcracker), longear, spotted sunfish (stumpknockers), and warmouth
- twenty-five black crappie (speckled perch)

Check the latest fishing regulations for updates on these rules before you fish (1-800-ASK-FISH).

# Adventure 6

## Freshwater Critter Collecting

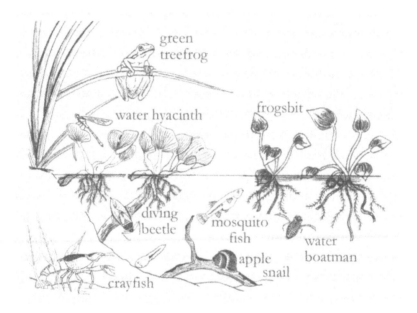

green treefrog

water hyacinth

frogsbit

diving beetle

mosquito fish

water boatman

apple snail

crayfish

Some people just don't have the patience or motivation to go fishing, but here's a kind of fishing that may be just perfect for us impetuous types. I call it "critter collecting."

The goal isn't to put food on the table, but then that's not always the purpose of traditional fishermen either. The satisfaction from the sport comes from catching and identifying as many different aquatic creatures as possible. Then you either return them to their watery home or build your very own, one-of-a-kind, native aquarium.

Very little investment is required to begin your new sport. All you need are a bucket and a small mesh dip net. An inexpensive field guide (such as *Pond Life* from the Golden Guide series) comes in handy for identifying your catch. Then put on your old sneakers, roll up your pantlegs, and head for the river, marsh, slough, swamp, lake, or ditch. The more types of wet places you dip in, the greater variety of animals you can catch.

The method is quite simple. Go to the wet place of your choice, such as the bank of the Myakka River where it flows through one of the picnic areas. Reach out and place the net in the deepest water you can reach from the shore. Drop the net down to the river bottom, then slowly drag it towards you. You will probably bring up quite a bit of plant life and mud. Dump the net close to the water's edge and use your fingers to sort through the mess to find your prey. Working close to the water's edge allows critters you miss to make their way back to the water. Dip in many different kinds of areas to get the greatest variety: a grassy area, open water, shallow water, and deeper water. Scrape the bottom and dip the surface. You will be surprised at the number of different creatures you find.

For instance, there are thirty-three species of fish common to the Myakka River area. The sunfish are the most colorful. Some are sparkling yellow or speckled orange. It is hard to distinguish among species, but you can always tell sunfish by their deep, rounded body shape. Shiners and flagfish are also pretty. Golden shiners have golden-brassy bodies with orange fins, and flagfish brandish alternating rows of red and bluish-green dots as their name implies. The tadpole madtom may be the ugliest fish. He is a little catfish no longer than five inches with large barbs and a Fu Manchu mustache.

Mosquito fish are the easiest to catch. If you capture only mosquito fish, you are dipping too close to the surface of the water. As their name implies, they are a beneficial fish to have around since they eat mosquito larvae. The females look like they're pregnant (or are big beer drinkers). Each sports a black spot on her belly. The males lack the protruding belly and spot but are similar enough to the females that you can tell they are the same species. Some say mosquito fish look like guppies.

My favorite catch is a tiny flounder called a hogchoker. It's flat with eyes on one side of its body. It usually feeds at the bottom of shallow estuaries, but young fish sometimes swim up into freshwater rivers. Lower Myakka Lake is a good place to look, especially in the summer when the water level is high.

The fish are just the beginning. There are hundreds of other kinds of creatures to discover. Many insects begin their lives in the water, changing body shape as they grow and molt into flying or crawling insects. Dragonflies, damselflies, mosquitoes, horseflies, and whirligig beetles all have larval stages that don't resemble the adults at all.

Aquatic creatures are often strange in appearance and behavior. Water striders, true to their name, actually walk across the surface of the water. Fisher spiders eat small fish. Apple snails have both lungs and gills. They breathe through gills underwater; when the water dries up, they burrow into the mud and use their lungs. Water scorpions look similar to the terrestrial insects known as walking sticks and are a favorite for both kids and adults. The long projectile that extends from the creature's body looks like a stinger but is actually a breathing tube that the animal raises to the water's surface (like a snorkel) for air.

Freshwater shrimp are a frequent catch. Their catapulting, iridescent bodies are fun to watch when placed in a small, inexpensive plastic aquarium. Some books call them grass shrimp (which tells you the best place to dip for them). Sometimes, if you're lucky, you can scoop up a crayfish or a colorful salamander, both considered unusual treasures by veteran dippers.

If you dip from mid to late summer, especially in ditches and small temporary ponds, you can find many kinds of tadpoles. In fact, there are some tadpoles that live only in small ponds that dry up in winter or spring. These ephemeral wetlands are not wet long enough to produce the big fish that prey on tadpoles. It is often difficult to distinguish among the different species of tadpoles, but you can discern young frogs from young toads by their color: toad tadpoles are jet black.

A few precautions will ensure a safe adventure for both you and your quarry. Use a rubber glove or a small hand net to handle fish. Touching fish with your fingers removes their protective coating, which can cause the growth of fungus that is deadly to the fish. Use the hand net for the big, black water beetles. They sting. Pick up crayfish carefully so they can't reach your fingers with their pinchers. If you have small children (say, under the age of eight), don't allow them to go to the water's edge alone. They may be small enough to be mistaken for a pig or deer by a hungry alligator. And, of course, never bring dogs or other pets anywhere close to the bank. Last of all, remember that it's illegal to catch and keep game fish caught by net. Game fish include bass, crappie, warmouth, bluegill, and sunfish.

## Fishing Wisdom

For well over a century, fishermen have been drawn to the Myakka River in anticipation of proving their skills. They have their own secret methods for enticing the "big one" and their own special places to fish. After you read this adventure, you'll be privy to advice provided by some of Myakka's oldest and most successful fishermen.

The oldest fisherman to share his methodology with me was Robert Johnson. He fished Deep Hole around 1910 with a reed and a piece of salt pork bacon cut like "legs" dangling from the sides. When he ran out of bacon, he'd cut a piece of his shirttail off and fashion a lure in the same way and still catch plenty of bass.

Another angler told me her favorite spot forty years ago was right in the middle of the railroad bridge that crossed the Myakka River. She could always catch enough speckled perch there to feed her entire

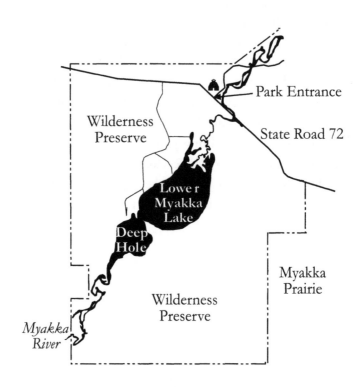

family. The railroad bridge over the river is gone now, but if you follow the power line west from Park Drive, you'll come to where the bridge used to be. People still fish there, even if they can't get out to the middle of river.

Park rangers would certainly say that Ernest Campbell earned the title of most successful fisherman long ago. Some folks catch fish when they're lucky. Some catch fish when they're skillful. Mr. Campbell catches fish *all* the time. If there were only two fish in the whole lake, he'd catch one of them.

Mr. Campbell's territory is the Upper Myakka Lake. He goes out in a small johnboat and fishes with earthworms for catfish, shellcrackers, and bluegill. "Don't let the end of the hook show," he cautioned me one day as he looped the huge earthworm back and forth, sticking it with the hook after each loop. "If you don't cover it up with the worm, the fish will see it and never bite." This legendary angler also advises, "the hotter it gets, the better the fishing; the best fishing comes when there's just a bit of chop to the water; if you don't catch fish within about fifteen minutes, just move to another spot; and when it gets really hot, the best place to throw your line is under the boat."

You may find that identifying your fish is harder than catching them. Books are fine for learning to identify the basic shapes, but I don't find the colors helpful at all. The best way to learn is from another fisherman. Here are a few hints to help get you started. Redear sunfish (shellcrackers) have an orange mark below the blue on the gill. Bluegills are similarly shaped, but they lack the orange spot. Specs, or black crappie, are covered with tiny, black spots. Three kinds of catfish live in the lake: yellow cats, speckled cats (bullhead), and the deep blue-gray channel cats. Be sure to bring some pliers to remove catfish from your hook; their barbs can be very intimidating.

Two fish that most people throw back are the long, thin garfish and the heavy-bodied mudfish, or bowfin. Mr. Campbell keeps the mudfish. He cleans and boils the fish, removes the bones, then chops the fish and mixes it with a bit of hamburger. From this mixture, he makes patties, which he fries.

And finally, four fish that you should never throw back: brown Hoplo (armored catfish), tilapia, vermiculated sailfin catfish, and walking catfish. It is illegal to release these four exotic invaders back into Florida waters. All are edible except the walking catfish. These accidental imports compete with native fish and ruin aquatic ecosystems. You'll find photos of them on the Myakka Wild & Scenic Trails Map and at the fish exhibit at the fishing pier by the weir at Upper Myakka Lake. ✄

# 3

# Gators Galore

Waist-high buttonbush shrubs obscured the view of a photograph I wanted to take to document changes in vegetation along the Myakka River. In 1976, some enterprising photographer had snapped a picture of the exact view depicted in a 1946-vintage photograph of the river. Now, as I attempted to produce the third photograph in the series twenty-two years later, the view was obscured by a few wax myrtles, young palms, and a group of buttonbush growing along the bank. I easily trimmed back the palms and myrtles with loppers, but when I reached the buttonbush I had to remove my shoes and wade ankle-deep into the water to continue the task.

As I lopped off the first half dozen sprouts, I noticed that each made a tinkling sound as it fell into the river. I imagined the sound was similar to a deer wading through the water, and I wondered if an alligator might be attracted by the sound. I stepped back and surveyed the shoreline. No alligators in sight. I decided I was being silly but changed my method of lopping. Now I grabbed each shrub after I cut it and turned and threw it onto the bank instead of allowing it to tinkle into the water. After depositing four or five shrubs on the bank, I turned back, and as I started to lean over to stretch the loppers out for the next shrub, I saw the snout of a twelve-foot alligator between my feet!

His massive, bony head protruded above the shallow water, but the rest of his body was hidden from view. He looked up at me with huge bulging eyes. I screamed. Immediately, the words of an alligator expert I had once interviewed came to mind. I had asked him what someone at risk of being attacked by an alligator should do. After reassuring me such a circumstance would be improbable, if not rare, he advised, "Never scream. A scream would imitate the sound made by an animal in distress—perfect prey for an alligator."

The gator lay still, staring up at me. I raised the loppers above my head and made myself appear as tall and huge as possible. Then I shouted, with the loudest, deepest voice I could muster, "Get out of here!" The gator turned and, with a tremendous splash, bolted at lighting speed back to the center of the river.

You may wonder why I'm telling you this story if my purpose is to alleviate your fear of alligators. Though I could have been seriously injured by that gator, I still believe that alligators are not dangerous if you understand and respect their natural instincts. I could have called this chapter Alligator Behavior 101 because here I will explain what I have come to understand about alligators during my years of exploring Myakka.

People often ask how fast an alligator can run. Alligators can move extremely fast in water and for short distances on land, but any fantastic claim you may hear about how many miles an hour an alligator can run is ridiculous. An alligator would never run a mile for anyone to clock. So any claim for speed would need to be expressed in feet per second rather than miles per hour.

Another question posed by park visitors is whether they can elude an alligator by running in a zigzag pattern. This theory is equally absurd. An alligator does not chase its prey. It strikes, snatches, and then submerges (often with a twisting motion) to drown large prey. When that alligator positioned himself between my feet, he did not make a sound, not a splash, not a hint of an approach. He came in so fast that he arrived in the time it took me to turn, place a branch on the shore, and turn back again. That is how an alligator feeds. A game biologist with Florida Fish and Wildlife who investigates alligator incidents told me that victims of serious alligator attacks rarely see the animal before the encounter.

In my encounter, the gator looked up and realized I was not his prey. He was as surprised to see a human towering above him as I was to see a gator staring up at me. The following day, I returned to the scene to contemplate calling a gator trapper and condemning a dangerous alligator to his death. The area was surrounded by tall grass and aquatic plants. The alligator could not have seen me before his approach. He had instinctively reacted only to the sounds he had heard. This was an alligator exhibiting natural behavior. I saw a package of hotdog buns floating in the river a few feet upstream and realized that my not-guilty verdict might be just a temporary reprieve for this gator. The most frequent reason we must call for the removal of an alligator is that it has been fed by humans. Alligators normally avoid or ignore humans, but a fed alligator will boldly approach people. To feed an alligator is to condemn it to death.

Sometimes wary potential campers will ask about their chances of encountering an alligator in the campground. It's as if they imagine a huge reptile stalking through the camp, pulling sleeping campers from their tents for a midnight snack. A typical ranger response would be, "Alligators only go into the campground if it is two feet underwater, when no one would be camping there." But one year a seven-foot alligator proved us wrong. It was a very dry spring and the gator's marsh had probably dried up. He was looking for water and his path to the lake took him right through the campground at mid-morning. Someone had propped the bathroom door open for the floor to dry. The gator, following the scent of water, took a detour right into the men's restroom. I would have bet anything that no one would ever find an alligator in a camp bathroom. But the story of how the ranger who responded to the call to get a seven-foot alligator out of a bathroom certainly goes on record as one of the most unique ranger tales at this park.

It is primarily this wanderlust for water in the dry spring that I have always believed is the reason alligators have a reputation for being aggressive during mating season. Each spring you'll read newspaper articles implying the dire consequences of encountering alligators during mating season. People even call to ask if it's safe to visit the park this time of the year. The main difference in alligator behavior in the spring, compared to other times of the year, is their increase in movement across land.

When wetlands are dry (which usually corresponds to the April/May mating season), alligators may travel for miles to find a wet home. Young alligators, chased out of wetlands by more dominant males, are also looking for new homes. People find alligators in their swimming pools or in subdivision culverts. A startled hiker may discover a six-footer sprawled across a hiking trail, resting up for the rest of his journey. I had never observed a Myakka alligator display what I would define as aggressive behavior until last spring.

I was on the riverbank with a camera and tripod, photographing river shots for a park brochure. Suddenly, an alligator zipped up to the edge of the water. I jumped up to the next level on the bank. At first I was annoyed at this bold, five-foot alligator for surprising me. I thought someone had been feeding him and so he had charged to the riverbank for a handout. Hoping to spare his life as he grew larger and expecting to teach him respect, I stomped, yelled, and charged towards him. But instead of retreating as I had expected him to do, he came right up onto the shore. Without hesitation, I backed off. I had suddenly realized that it was April—mating season. The alligator's abrupt approach was a message that this was his territory and I was intruding. When I charged him, I was challenging him for it. He was simply telling me he was willing to fight for his territory if necessary. I decided to take my photos farther downstream.

I think alligators are among Myakka's most fascinating creatures. Even after analyzing their behavior, learning about their amazing adaptations for survival, and discovering the story of their ecology, I don't think I could ever tire of learning all there is to know about these reptiles. Their bodies are engineered so perfectly for their environment that they were even able to return from the brink of extinction. In cold temperatures, alligators can survive months without food and hours without air. They have built-in diving gear: flaps that close over their ears and nose to keep out water when they dive; transparent shields to cover their eyes like goggles; and webbed feet like swim fins. They even have a specialized valve in their throat called a glottis that enables them to capture their prey underwater without drowning. (To swallow, however, alligators must lift their heads out of the water.)

I've read that an alligator's brain is so small that it is not capable of cognitive thought processes such as those of primates, cats, and dogs. Since alligators rely completely on instinct, reacting only to immediate stimuli, they can't be trained (which is why they can't be kept as pets). But one day I was burning a small island in the river and noticed about three or four alligators congregating at the edge of one end of the island. I watched them, wondering why they were gathering there. The fire burned slowly across the strip of land. When it reached the corner where the gators were lingering, several rabbits jumped into the water. Each reptile caught his dinner and moved away from the burned island.

The alligator's life history is equally intriguing. Early mornings in April and May, you can hear the bellows that signify mating season has begun. I equate the sound to someone's attempting to pull-start an outboard motor that won't quite catch. Surprisingly, alligators don't have vocal chords. Those lionlike roars are produced by the way an alligator manipulates air through its throat.

In June or July, females meticulously construct large mounds of vegetation along lake edges and marshes in which to lay their eggs. About twenty to forty-five eggs are deposited at varying levels throughout the pile of vegetation. The mound is heated by decaying vegetation and the rays of the sun. It is the temperature at which the eggs incubate that determines the sex of the hatchlings. Cooler layers (82–86° F) produce females, warmer layers (90–93° F) produce males, and those in between produce both sexes. The incubation period is about sixty-five days. During this time the female alligator usually guards her nest against intruders, though studies reveal that, just like humans, some mothers perform their maternal roles better than others. Eggs usually hatch from August through September.

I once read a study demonstrating that alligators actually communicate with each other before they hatch. A researcher took eggs from two different nests. One group of eggs was laid two weeks prior to the other. When the first set of eggs began to hatch, grunts produced by alligators still inside the eggs not only prompted all of the siblings to hatch, but also induced animals from the younger batch to hatch. None of the premature alligators survived.

People usually think of alligators as large predators whose only role in nature is to control the populations of their prey. But the alligator actually plays such an important part in Florida's ecosystem that it is considered a keystone species, one whose presence or absence has a profound effect on the rest of a natural community. Alligators are not only predators but are also prey themselves when they're still small. Predators include raccoons, wading birds, snakes, ospreys, otters, large bass, garfish, and larger alligators. Once an alligator reaches about four feet, its only predators are humans and, occasionally, larger alligators.

During the dry season, alligators excavate low areas of small seasonal ponds and marshes, preventing them from drying up. These ephemeral wetlands are often the only source of water in an area and are essential to the survival of wildlife throughout dry spring.

Alligators feed upon "trash" fish such as gars, which are natural predators of young game fish like bass. Alligator excrement was probably once very valuable to Florida's naturally nutrient-deficient lakes and rivers.

If you spend much time in Myakka, you are sure to encounter many of these awesome reptiles. You can observe them without fear by using a little common sense. For instance, don't approach within three feet of a large bull alligator and bend over to take a close-up photograph. Don't approach an alligator's nest or try to pick up a hatchling. And don't walk your dog to the river's edge for a drink. Unbelievably, I have encountered park visitors engaged in each of these activities.

Here are some safety tips for traveling in alligator habitat. Be careful when wading through lakes, rivers, swamps, marshes, and ditches, especially in cold weather. Alligators are most likely to be submerged when the temperature drops. There are several reports of people who were bitten after stepping on an alligator. Don't allow small children to play along the river's banks or in shallow water. They are not large enough for an alligator to distinguish from normal prey such as deer. And help spread the word. If you see a stranger feeding an alligator, take a moment to explain that it's not only dangerous but illegal to feed alligators in the wild.

Alligators are not only fascinating creatures but a vital part of our ecosystem as well. People and alligators can coexist without peril if people simply respect the needs and instincts of alligators and give them a bit of space.

## Gator Questions and Answers

- *How big is Myakka's largest alligator?*
  Since alligators have been protected here for over six decades, Myakka should have some of our state's largest alligators. But since the only time an alligator is actually measured is when it is no longer alive, there's no way to determine the length of the park's largest reptile. The park's largest alligator could be about fourteen feet long. Adult male alligators usually weigh between 180 and 228 kg (400–500 lbs.).

- *How can I estimate the length of an alligator?*
  The number of inches between the eyes and the tip of the nose is

roughly equal to an alligator's length in feet.

- *How old is Myakka's oldest alligator?*

    Alligators in the wild are believed to live thirty-five to fifty years. In captivity they may live sixty to eighty years. Currently, there are no scientific methods to estimate an alligator's age while it is alive. Young alligators grow about one foot a year until they are about six feet long. This six-year period is the only time a rough estimate of age is practical.

    Recently, Harry McVay, one of this book's illustrators, told me he had just seen a large alligator with one eye that he had photographed in 1972. I explained how unlikely it was that it was the same alligator, especially since I know of two large, one-eyed alligators that have been removed from the park. He insisted it was the same alligator because the one he photographed in 1972 also had a cleft snout. I was still skeptical that a large, old alligator seen in 1972 was still swimming in the river today, but, coincidentally, a park volunteer photographed a large alligator with one eye and a cleft snout basking in the sun at the weir the same week.

- *What do alligators eat?*

    Young alligators feed on small fish, aquatic insects, frogs, snails, and crustaceans. Adults eat fish, turtles, wading birds, ducks, snakes, frogs, small mammals, and even smaller alligators. Examinations of alligators' stomachs have also found such objects as stones, sticks, cans, and fishing lures.

- *Why do alligators bask in the sun with their mouths open?*

    Alligators regulate their body temperature by basking in the sun to warm up, by opening their mouths to cool slightly, by diving into cool water to cool more, and by tunneling into riverbanks to avoid freezing temperatures.

- *Where do alligators live?*
  The only places in the world you can find alligators in the wild are in the southeastern United States and in the Yangtze River Basin in China.

- *How many alligators live in the park?*
  Florida Fish and Wildlife Conservation Commission biologists occasionally conduct night counts in the Upper Lake and the river between the lake and S.R. 72. Over the past two decades, the number of alligators counted on one night during these surveys has ranged between 134 and 388 individuals. Of course, these counts don't include alligators in other parts of the river, Lower Lake, or the thousands of wetlands scattered throughout the park's forty-five square miles. It would be almost impossible to estimate the number of alligators in the park or in the Myakka Island.

- *How can you tell a male from a female alligator?*
  There is no way to distinguish the sexes visually. However, an alligator guarding a nest is most likely a female. An alligator over nine feet long is usually a male.

- *How can I tell if I am looking at an alligator or a crocodile?*
  If you're in Myakka, it's an alligator. Crocodiles are not found north of Naples in the wild. Alligators have rounded snouts while crocodiles have longer, pointed snouts.

- *How many teeth does an alligator have?*
  There are approximately eighty teeth in the mouth at one time. As they wear down, they are replaced. An alligator can go through two thousand to three thousand teeth in a lifetime.

- *How far does an alligator travel over land?*
  An alligator doesn't usually travel over land unless something forces it to leave its wetland. During mating season, competition

with larger alligators often drives younger ones to find new territory. When wetlands dry up, an alligator that can no longer excavate to reach water looks for a new home. I have followed gator tracks for over two miles along the railroad grade until the road became too grassy to see the tracks.

- *How long can an alligator hold its breath?*
  In cold weather, an alligator can sit at the bottom of the river for hours. But when the temperature is higher and alligators are active, they must breathe every few minutes. I once read that Ross Allen, a famous reptile handler known for wrestling alligators, could stay underwater longer than an alligator during a strenuous performance.

- *Has anyone ever been attacked by an alligator in the park?*
  There have been no serious injuries resulting from an alligator attack. In the early 1960s a man wading in the river off the west end of the power line with a stringer of fish attached to his belt was bitten on the leg, probably in an attempt to take the fish. Another bite occurred at Deep Hole in the late '60s. The victim, another fisherman, told me that a twelve-foot alligator had been loitering in the area all day and was being fed by another group of people. The gator clamped onto the fisherman's leg as he was wading into the lake. Though he believed the bite occurred because the gator had previously been fed, he may have stepped on or near the submerged alligator, causing a reflex reaction; or since the attack occurred in April and resulted in only two puncture wounds, it may have been the alligator's attempt to reclaim territory. In 2002 I was bitten on my leg while removing exotic grasses from a small wetland. Another ranger and I had inadvertently trapped the unseen gator between us.

- *Is it true that alligators are especially attracted to dogs?*
  Yes. Some alligator experts believe that some of the alligator attacks on record may have occurred because the gator was

attracted to the scent of a dog in close proximity to the victim. The park has several accounts of dogs being attacked by alligators, so it's important to keep all pets away from bodies of water, including ditches and culverts under roadways.

- *Is Old Charlie the Alligator still out at the park?*
  Old Charlie is immortal. He has been at the park since I was a child, and, unless something catastrophic occurs in Myakka, your great-grandchild's youngest child will still find him there. Charlie is over twelve feet long and sometimes described as having only one eye. He can be found at the bridge or the boat basin, depending on the latest claim of his territory. What's his secret to eternal life? When a large alligator claims territory, no other alligator dares intrude. When Charlie expires, another large alligator moves in to take his territory, indistinguishable from the previous Charlie by park visitors.

## Adventure 1

## Gator Watching

If you come to Myakka to watch alligators, there are very few days that you will have any difficulty locating your quarry. The only time you may not be able to find them is when it's too hot, too cold, or too windy.

The best time to spot alligators is when the temperature is cool enough to bring them out onto the banks to sun but warm enough to allow their bodies to function normally. Since alligators are cold-blooded and their body heat is completely dependent upon their environment, you won't usually see them out when the temperature drops below 65° or so. When the air temperature decreases, an alligator's heartbeat and metabolism slow down so it can sink into warm water and remain submerged for many hours without breathing. Or it can back into a gator cave dug along the banks of a river, lake, or marsh. Cave openings are often underwater, making them impossible to see until the water levels drop significantly. Alligator caves are much more common further north than they are in central and south Florida.

When it is very hot, alligators stay submerged in the cooler water with only their eyes and noses above the water's surface, making them more difficult to locate. Also, since the marshes are full of summer rain during hot weather, alligators are no longer concentrated in the river and lakes.

Many people take the concessionaire's airboat tours specifically to see alligators. The boat captains do a great job stalking the lake's resident crocodilians even when conditions are less favorable for gator watching. But there are plenty of places to look for alligators without taking the tours. North Drive, which winds along the lakeshore, is often a good place to look, as is the birdwalk. Take a walk to Alligator Point (see directions in the Shady Walks adventure in Chapter 7) or walk back to the river behind the log pavilion. The park bridge is a favorite gator hangout, as is the weir behind the concession. If you don't find them in any of these places, that means it is too cold or too windy for gator watching. Come back another day.

But before you leave the area, test your "gator I.Q." at the alligator exhibit located at the fishing pier, beside the weir at Upper Myakka Lake. Paula Sharpe, a local artist, contributed some terrific illustrations for it and Sierra Club financed the fabrication of this unique display. But what makes it so extraordinary are the sounds that come with this interactive exhibit. Ackerman Computer Sciences, a local company in Sarasota that designs and builds digital message audio repeaters, created an innovative sound system that seems to bring the attraction to life. After testing your knowledge with a true and false trivia game you can push a button to hear the difference between the sound of a pig frog and a baby alligator calling for its mother. Another button will summon the call of an adult alligator bellowing to impress a mate. ✦

# 4

# Fire, Most Naturally

*Belinda Perry contributed to the writing of this chapter.*

"Continued sunny and warm except for isolated afternoon or evening thunderstorms. Sixty percent chance of rain."

You hear this forecast almost every day during the summer in Florida. And with thunderstorms comes lightning. There is more lightning in central Florida than anyplace else in North America, so for thousands of years fires ignited by lightning have skipped across pine flatwoods, prairies, and wetlands every spring and summer. All the plants and animals that live in these habitats have evolved over the centuries to depend on fire for their survival. Nature has developed a perfect system for rejuvenation: lightning supplies the ignition source, wind carries the fire, and rain puts the fires out. It is the frequency of these fires combined with climate and terrain that determines what lives on every inch of soil in our state.

Fire-dependent communities are prevalent in Myakka. Seventy-eight percent of the park and eighty-one percent of the adjoining Myakka Prairie must burn frequently to remain healthy. Until about seventy years ago, fires came regularly, ignited by lightning or Native Americans. A fire could burn for days before arriving at what is now park land: rambling across prairies, winding around wetlands too wet to burn, pausing overnight when the humidity climbed, then, rekindled by wind and sun the next day, continuing its journey. But now lightning fires that occur in populated areas must be quickly extinguished. If we relied only on fires ignited within park boundaries, the frequency of fire would not be high enough for fire-dependent plants and animals to survive. So every year, park rangers plan and conduct prescribed burns. Though the preferred time to burn is in the spring and early summer, when most natural fires burned historically, we also plan some fires for the dormant season so we can accomplish yearly burn objectives.

Myakka was acquired in 1934, a time when "protection" meant suppressing fires at the first whiff of smoke. I imagine that with over a hundred diligent CCC workers "protecting" Myakka, there weren't many acres burned in those early years. The more accessible an area was to firefighting equipment, the less likely lightning fires were able to burn.

It wasn't until the 1970s that park managers began to understand the concept of fire-dependent habitats and to reintroduce fire by way of "controlled burns." Of course, as rough as the vegetation had become after so many years of fire exclusion, those early fires were not always very "controlled."

In the years that followed, as park managers began to discover the needs of Myakka's fire-dependent acreage, the preferred burn season was shifted from the traditional dormant season (winter) to the growing season (late spring and summer) to mimic natural lightning fires. Managers also began to apply fires more frequently as they gained insight into historic fire cycles. Restoring Myakka's fire-dependent acreage was a slow, assiduous process. Some areas were in much worse condition than others, and the park's land managers soon realized that fire alone may not be adequate to restore long-unburned areas to their natural state. They also realized that some areas had degraded so much that they might never return to the condition they were in prior to fire exclusion.

It is an understatement to say that working in a natural area as large and diverse as Myakka River State Park is a rewarding experience. There is something new to discover every single day. But the most intriguing and fascinating facet of my job is, without a doubt, involvement with fire ecology. From planning and executing burns, to observing and learning about fire behavior, to monitoring and documenting effects of fire, to researching and collecting data on a never-ending list of intricacies in the story of fire, I continue to find the subject amazing. The entire life cycle of every single organism in Florida's fire-dependent communities is innately linked to natural fire cycles. It's like an intricate puzzle with every piece fitting just right.

One of the most common questions people ask about fire is, What happens to the animals when a fire burns across the landscape? Most people picture singed fur, death, and devastation. If you think about it, though, you soon realize this would be completely illogical. Any species of animal that lives in an area dependent on frequent fire would not live there if it had not developed a way to avoid the flames.

Most natural fires in Florida are not particularly fast moving or very hot. Frequent fires prevent the buildup of thick vegetation that would cause hot fires. Large animals have no problem moving out of the path of a fire under natural conditions. Smaller animals often go underground or move to areas too wet to burn, such as marshes or depressions in the landscape. Birds simply fly away and often return as soon as the flames pass. After a natural fire, the landscape is a mosaic of burned and unburned areas, with animals moving from one to the other according to their needs. Many animals are even drawn to a fire to seek prey that has been flushed out by the flames or is easier to spot in the blackened area, to glean seeds made easier to locate, and even to lick the mineral salts contained in the ash.

Plants and animals of fire-dependent lands (such as pinelands, prairies, and marshes) have special adaptations that allow them to live in these areas. Some of these adaptations are easily observed and others are more subtle. For example, when you walk through a pine forest, the scent of pine trees fills the air. Some of the compounds that produce "piney" odors are very flammable. Pine trees, wax myrtles, saw palmettos, and many other plants have volatile oils that help carry fire across the landscape, yet the thick bark of most pines insulates them from the heat of the flames. Some even have cones that do not open until heated by fire. Here are some other examples of how plants and animals adapt to fire. There are hundreds more. There is always something new to discover. But, then, that is what makes fire so interesting.

- Longleaf pine seedlings remain grasslike for up to seven years as they put their energy into developing a strong root system. Burned under natural conditions, this grasslike stage usually survives. When the root system is well developed, the grasslike pine quickly sprouts up into a young tree, towering over ground vegetation in a season's time. As long as the area burns often enough to keep groundcover low, the pine easily survives each passing fire.

- Saw palmettos and cabbage palms appear to be completely consumed by fire, but they quickly regrow fronds from the heart, which is unharmed by the blaze.

- Grasses, blueberries, and runner oaks store their energy in their roots so they easily resprout and often grow fast enough to flower and fruit by fall.

- The nesting period of Florida scrub jays, turkeys, bald eagles, and many other birds is timed to coincide with the natural fire season. Chicks fledge before the late spring and summer fires. The freshly burned areas are abundant with food for the growing birds, which increases survival rates for the young.

- The endangered red-cockaded woodpecker must have mature pines with low undergrowth in order to survive, a condition that exists only in areas of frequent fire.

- Gopher tortoises eat low-growing, tender grasses and herbs that are prevalent for several years after a fire. With their squat profile, these grazers must have succulent food available within twelve inches from the ground. Their burrows provide a haven for many other animals during fires as well.
- Florida soil is poor in nutrients and so sandy that what nutrients are available quickly leech out. Fire provides plants with the fertilizers they need in order to grow and reproduce.
- Fire transfers nitrogen from the leaf litter to the soil and increases potassium, calcium, phosphorus, and magnesium. It also raises the pH of Florida's otherwise acidic soils.
- Fire stimulates flower and seed production; scarifies seeds (breaks the outer seed covering) so they can germinate; prepares a warm, nutrient-enriched seedbed; and maintains an open canopy so seedlings can get more sunlight.
- By reducing shrub height and density, fire encourages an abundance of grasses and herbaceous plants, which in turn increases the number of insects, rodents, and other small mammals an area can support. Small animals are the basis of the food supply of predatory animals like hawks, snakes, and bobcats.
- In dry years, fire clears marshes of vegetation buildup to improve their ability to store water.

# Adventure 1

# Bee Island Loop

You can experience Myakka's fire-dependent habitats in various stages of restoration by hiking or bicycling the Bee Island Loop. It will probably take you most of the day to hike the 10.7-mile hiking trail loop, or you can hike or bike the 8.9-mile dirt road Loop. Pick up a hike/bike map at the Ranger Station and remember to take a compass and plenty of water for this adventure. Bring your own bicycle or rent one from the park concession.

To hike the trail, begin at Fox's Low Road on North Park Drive. Take Fox's Low Road about two-tenths of a mile to the trailhead. Take the trail north to where it splits and you can choose either the trail to Mossy Hammock campsite or the one to Bee Island. The trail to Mossy is the east side of the loop and will take you in a clockwise direction around the loop, through Bee Island, and back to the trailhead. The east part of the trail is about half shaded. The rest of the hike to Bee Island is in open sun. The prairie, wetlands, and pinelands on the east side of the loop are in the best condition, as is evident by the diverse, grassy, and herbaceous groundcover; the stunted, scattered shrubs; and the low density of palmetto.

The trail to Bee Island is the west side of the loop and will take you counterclockwise along the route. It passes through a variety of habitats, in and out of shade on its way to Bee Island. Head-high palmetto and shrubs, oak trees with a thick palmetto groundcover, and a lack of grasses and other herbs are all indicators of degraded, fire-excluded habitat. You are most likely to encounter these conditions closest to Park Drive.

To bicycle or walk the dirt road loop, begin at Fox's High Road.

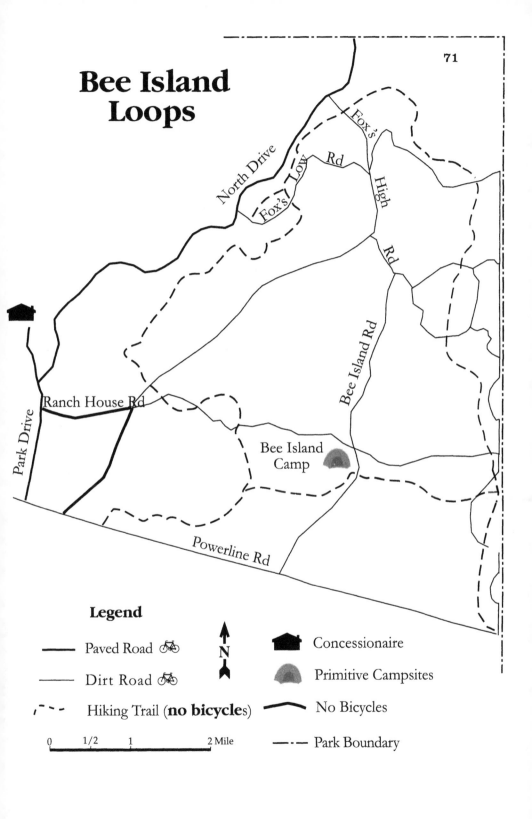

# Bee Island Loops

North Drive

Fox's

Fox's Low Rd

High Rd

Fox's Low

Bee Island Rd

Ranch House Rd

Park Drive

Bee Island Camp

Powerline Rd

## Legend

—— Paved Road 🚲

—— Dirt Road 🚲

- - - Hiking Trail (**no bicycles**)

🏠 Concessionaire

Primitive Campsites

⌒ No Bicycles

—··— Park Boundary

N

0   1/2   1   2 Mile

Take the High Road to All Weather Road, go south to Bee Island Road, then turn left onto Bee Island Road and take it to Ranch House Road. The prairie and pinelands along Bee Island Road should be in good condition. Turn right onto Ranch House Road and head west. You'll pass the entrance to Bee Island campground a few feet from the intersection of Bee Island and Ranch House Roads.

The prairie along the north side of Ranch House Road (on your left) has a natural abundance of grasses and herbs. Some years, following prescribed fires, the fall wildflower bloom is spectacular. Then the prairie is full of bright-orange pine lilies, Indian grass, purple members of the aster family, and a rare species of ground orchid *(Pteroglossapsis ecristata)*. Ranch House Road leaves the prairie, goes through shady hammock and past some massive wetlands that were once known as Sumeral Ponds (see Chapter 7). Next you'll pass through some tall, thick palmetto with an oak overstory evident of a history of fire exclusion. Take a right turn when you reach All Weather Road and follow it for 3.1 miles to Fox's High Road. Fox's High Road will take you back to your point of origin.

# $A^{dventur}e$ 2

## Seeking the "Pinelands Landlord"

**Gopher tortoise**

The gopher tortoise is one of Florida's longest-living animals. During the 80–150 years it spends in this world, it contributes to the survival of countless species of plants and animals. This unique reptile tunnels into the sandy soil, excavating an underground burrow up to thirty feet long. The tortoise spends most of its life in its tunnel, safe from the intense Florida sun, the cold, the dry days of winter, and the frequent fires so common in the pinewoods.

More than eighty different animals are known to take up residence or seek shelter inside gopher tortoise burrows. The threatened indigo snake and the endangered Florida mouse and gopher frog all depend on these subterranean dwellings for survival. Bobwhite quails, burrowing owls, and wrens are frequent visitors, and during a fire an assortment of snakes, mice, rats, lizards, and opossums can all be found in the shelter waiting for the flames to pass.

Some insects spend their entire lives in gopher tortoise burrows and provide food for other burrow visitors. The piles of bare sand at the entrance to the burrows are frequented by mole skinks: lizards that require bare, sandy areas for "sand swimming." The tortoise is also a disperser of seeds, preserving the diversity of plants that grow in its territory.

Newly hatched gopher tortoises look very different from their ancient, dull-gray parents. They are bright black and yellow and less than two inches long. The little fellows grow only about one half inch per year and take more than a decade to reach maturity. You can estimate the age of a young tortoise by counting the growth rings around the scutes of its shell, just like you would count the rings on a tree. This works only until the animal is about thirty years old, however, since the rings fade with age.

This slow-moving, stately animal was once abundant in dry, sandy pine flatwoods and scrubs from Florida to South Carolina. But in recent years its population has declined so quickly that it is now considered a listed species. (Listed species are plants and animals listed as endangered, threatened, or species of special concern.)

In years past, people considered the tortoise a readily available food source. Gopher stew, gopher eggs, fried gopher—dinner was as close as the nearest pineywoods. Then, when people tried to rid the landscape of rattlesnakes by pouring gasoline into tortoise burrows, tortoises were exterminated right along with the snakes and whatever else happened to be in the burrows at the time.

Today, loss of habitat is by far the greatest threat to these distinguished reptiles. Their well-drained, timbered uplands are prime locations for agriculture and for housing developments. What the bulldozer misses is often ruined by fire exclusion. Without frequent fires, shrubs and trees grow profusely, shading out the tender grasses and herbs that turtles graze. Roads and highways built through the remaining patches of native habitat also take a heavy toll on the slow-moving turtles. Tortoise roadkills are especially high in the spring during breeding season, when adult tortoises travel long distances.

As if all this weren't enough, a fatal respiratory disease that affects tortoises has become widespread. It is so contagious that it can wipe out an entire population of gopher tortoises within a short period of time. Wildlife biologists have traced the spread of the epidemic to well-meaning people who try to rescue turtles from recently transformed urban landscapes by transferring them to their native habitat. These natural areas already support as many tortoises as the land can sustain, so when the additional animals arrive, overcrowding leads to stress and makes turtles more susceptible to disease. As habitat destruction increases, diseased turtles are moved to new areas and healthy tortoises are exposed to the affliction.

Gopher tortoises are still common here at Myakka. They are among the easiest of Myakka's wildlife to observe and photograph. As long as you don't approach them too closely, they will obliviously continue their daily rituals. Dry pinewoods such as the Bee Island area are the best kinds of places to look for them. You can find them grazing close to their burrows in the early morning and late afternoon.

I believe you can predict when tortoises will be most active by checking the time of moonrise and moonset. I find them out grazing both when the moon is high in the sky and halfway between moonset and moonrise. Marjorie Kinnan Rawlings, author of *The Yearling*, used the term "south moon under" to describe the latter time period. To find south moon under, count the number of hours between moonset and moonrise. Divide the number in half and add that to moonset. For instance, if moonset is 9:00 A.M. and moonrise is 8:00 P.M., look for tortoises around 2:30 P.M.

# Adventure 3

## Bicycling Fox's Loop

When Jim Fox began the first Myakka Wildlife Tours in the mid-1960s, one of the routes he chose for the tram tour included some old dirt roads on the north end of the park. The road farthest north became known as Fox's High Road, and the southern part of the route was called Fox's Low Road. So, although it is certain that furry, bushy-tailed animals by the same name use this route, they are not the source for the road names.

This adventure, under the right conditions, is a leisurely one-hour trip. You can combine it with a ride along North Drive to Clay Gully or a walk out onto the birdwalk to make an enjoyable morning or late afternoon excursion. The loop is about half sun, half shade. If you ride it from the High Road to the Low Road, you are less likely to take a wrong turn.

It's easiest to explain the right conditions by describing the wrong conditions. You expect dirt roads to be harder to pedal than a paved drive and there are times during the year when the loop can be formidable. When summer rains accumulate, the road is inundated with several inches of water. Conversely, in winter or spring it can get so dry that short sections of the road are transformed into "sugar sand," infamous for hampering travel by any wheeled vehicle.

Holes created by hog rooting are another peril you may encounter on the park's dirt roads. Feral hogs, domesticated animals gone wild, were brought to this country centuries ago and have wreaked havoc in natural areas ever since. Not only do they proliferate unimpeded by any natural predators and disrupt the food chain by preying on the food sources of native animals, their digging disturbs

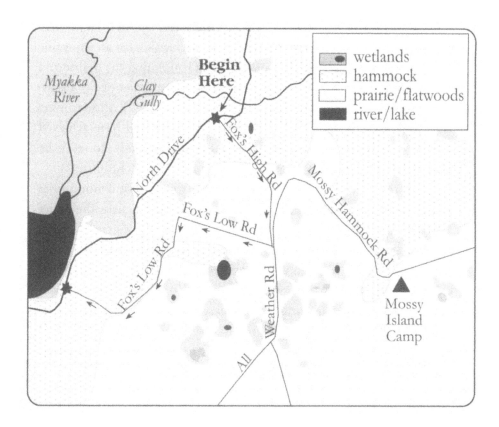

the soil layers, which changes the plant species that can grow there, and creates an obstacle course for unsuspecting bicyclists. The park's hog contractor routinely removes these nuisance animals, but the pigs are so numerous and prolific it is unlikely they will ever be eradicated from the park. When acorns or palmetto berries are on the ground, hog rooting is common along park roads.

Finally, you may encounter disked roads any time of the year. Service roads are used as fire breaks when park rangers conduct ecological burns. Burn preparation includes disking the road along the boundaries of the acreage to be burned. Tilled roads are definitely not compatible with bicycle travel. Rangers working in the office may not know which roads have been tilled, so it's best to simply alter your route when you discover these conditions.

As you travel around Fox's Loop, you'll pass through hammock, prairie, and flatwoods. The route is diverse and makes for an enjoyable trip. Casual visitors to the park often do not realize that the prairie and flatwoods along this loop were changed by many years of fire exclusion, as were other upland areas close to Park Drive. Park personnel have been restoring the area since the early 1980s and have achieved striking results. However, some sections are unlikely to ever be returned to the condition they were in prior to fire exclusion.

You can learn to appraise the health of the natural communities as you pedal through them. Usually, the grassier the prairie, the better its condition. Healthy prairies should have a nice mix of grasses, herbs, and low shrubs. Prior to restoration, most of the palmettos and other shrubs along this route grew over six feet tall and were so thick that animals couldn't even walk through them. To evaluate shady hammocks, remember that a true hammock does not have a solid understory of palmetto. When you discover a hammock with palmetto under the oak trees and can pick out an occasional big, old pine tree, you know pine flatwoods once grew there. &#x2766;

# 5

# Natural Communities

As you explore Myakka, the key to making the most interesting discoveries is developing an awareness of what belongs and what doesn't. You can enjoy the rewards of learning how to "read the land" no matter where you explore. This skill can increase your chances of locating a particular kind of animal; give you the ability to choose the easiest route when traveling cross-country (leaving trails and using a compass to navigate across native land); help you find your way when you are lost; and provide insight into the history of the land you explore. So where do you begin? The first and most important step is learning to recognize and understand the natural communities.

When I was first introduced to the concept of natural communities, it was a profound experience—sort of like discovering one of the secrets of the meaning of life. I learned that certain plants and animals naturally occurred together under specific conditions. Nature has a logical order, and the better I came to see how this intricate puzzle all fit together, the more pleasure I got from discovering new pieces.

Though this concept has been understood by outdoorsmen for centuries, the problem has been that there's no uniform terminology to describe these natural places. Do you explore the woods? The forest? The hammock? The bush? There is a nationwide trend to choose names for specific kinds of places. Here in Florida there is more than one organization involved in describing natural communities. The result is that we have several synonyms for many of our natural communities. Often the difference is in how specific the description is. For instance, you may call the shady habitat of palms and oaks you see along Park Drive a hammock. Or you could use the more specific name that the Florida Natural Areas Inventory (FNAI) chooses to describe it—a prairie hammock. As you can see, some classification systems are more complicated than others.

The natural communities in Myakka are pine flatwoods, scrubby flatwoods, dry prairie, hammock, swamp, marsh, river, and lake. Terrain and frequency of fire, combined with local climate, determine the occurrence of these natural areas throughout the region. Pine flatwoods, dry prairie, and marsh are the fire-dependent habitats.

Pine flatwoods is an upland community. In its natural state it is easily identified by widely spaced pine trees, low palmettos, and a fantastic variety of grasses, herbs, and shrubs. Unfortunately, there aren't many areas of pine flatwoods that have burned with natural frequency over the past few decades.

The pine flatwoods in lower elevations in the park is deemed mesic flatwoods by FNAI. Mesic flatwoods floods for short periods of time after heavy rains. It has gray, sandy soil and plants that are not quite as drought resistant as those found in higher flatwoods elevations. Though Myakka's pine flatwoods can have either longleaf or slash pines, the areas with longleaf pines are higher and drier than those composed primarily of slash pines. How can you distinguish slash pines from longleaf? Pick up a few needles from the ground. You will find that the needles are in bundles of two with an occasional bunch of three (slash pines) or in bundles of three with an occasional bunch of four (longleaf pines). The best example of mesic pine flat-woods is Bee Island.

Scrubby flatwoods is higher and drier than mesic flatwoods. The soil is white sugar-sand, and the plants have adapted to desertlike conditions. Leaves of many of the plants are tiny, waxy, spiny, succulent, curled under, or needlelike to conserve moisture. Longleaf pines dominate the overstory while scrub oaks with scattered shrubs fill the understory. Gopher tortoises, scrub jays, redheaded woodpeckers, nighthawks, cottontail rabbits, and towhees are common. You can find examples of scrubby flatwoods out near Oak Grove Camp, the northwest corner of the park, and along a ridge that crosses S.R. 72 northwest of Lower Myakka Lake.

The larger the variety of plants found in a natural community, the greater the diversity of animal life. Great horned owls, chuck-will's-widows, ground doves, fox squirrels, red-cockaded woodpeckers, Eastern towhees, gopher tortoises, cottontail rabbits, rattlesnakes, many kinds of warblers, red-tailed hawks, and bald eagles favor healthy pine flatwoods. Myakka lost red-cockaded woodpeckers during the decades of fire exclusion, but as restoration efforts progress we hope we can list them as park residents again someday.

Florida dry prairie is the community that requires the most frequent fire regime. Researchers believe that our prairies probably burned every one to three years before people began to suppress fire. Plants and animals that thrive in prairies depend upon this short fire cycle. The little Florida grasshopper sparrow, which is endemic to dry prairie, won't breed when an area goes for more than two years without fire. The presence of grasshopper sparrows is used to gauge the health of their habitat since they are the primary indicator of pristine conditions. Some wildflowers bloom only during the first two years after a fire.

Myakka's prairies tend to stay wetter longer than its pinelands. Plants like bachelor's button, yellow-eyed grass, and marsh pinks (usually found growing on wetland edges) flourish in some patches of dry prairie. Since pine flatwoods and dry prairies share some of the same species of plants (although in different proportions), some people believe it is the frequency of fire and the amount of inundation that discourages pines and produces dwarf versions of pinelands shrubs. Animals that share the prairie with grasshopper sparrows are caracaras, burrowing owls, and sandhill cranes. Most pinelands animals also live in or visit dry prairie.

Swamps, marshes, the river, and two shallow lakes make up Myakka's wetlands. What's the difference between swamps and marshes? Swamps have trees. They develop in places that seldom burn. Some classification systems refer to swamps as forested wetlands. An interesting example of a swamp is the cypress swamp in the Wilderness Preserve, west of Lower Lake. It is located nearly due south of the entrance to Myakka Valley Ranches subdivision. (See "Shady Walks" in Chapter 7).

All of Myakka's wetlands were formed as shallow single or multiple sinkholes. The marshes are open, sunny, and dominated by herbs and grasses. They are far more common than swamps due to Myakka's historic fire frequency and the sandy nature of their soils. Thousands of isolated marshes dot the prairies and pinelands, all of whose edges burn when the surrounding uplands burn. In the driest years many of these shallow wetlands dry up completely, allowing the entire marsh to burn. Some are as tiny as a quarter of an acre; others are massive, winding around hammocks or forming reflecting double teardrops across the landscape. Prairie ponds, flatwoods ponds, and seasonal ponds are all synonyms for isolated marshes.

Marshes that line the river corridor or abut the Upper and Lower Myakka Lakes are called floodplain marshes. Most of them are quite shallow and very grassy. Unfortunately, exotic grasses have invaded Myakka's floodplain marshes and have completely displaced native vegetation in some areas. Even if funding were available to purchase herbicides to eliminate these invasive grasses in the park, control would be futile unless a method was found to treat the entire river corridor. Perhaps the only hope would be to develop a biological control that could be released along the entire river. For now, the strategy is to prevent the grasses from invading the isolated marshes.

Sometimes marshes, swamps, or a combination of both form a chain of wetlands in which water actually flows towards a river, lake, or bay during the wet season. These chains of wetlands are called sloughs. Deer Prairie Slough crosses the railroad grade about five miles east of Park Drive and flows to the lower Myakka River in Venice. The section of the slough at the railroad grade is a beautiful forested wetland (or swamp) full of oaks, maples, tupelo, ash, and willow. The FNAI classification for this treed wetland is hydric hammock.

Three decades ago Deer Prairie Slough was the site of a large rookery. The Myakka Wildlife Tours tram was originally built to bring park visitors to a clearing just west of the slough where a tower had been erected to observe the birds. In the 1970s the slough began to dry up and the wading birds no longer returned each spring to nest. The tram's owner chose a new route, and when the tower began to deteriorate, it was dismantled and burned. Eventually a cycle of wet years brought the birds back to the area to nest. Now herons and egrets use the rookery during wet years and choose other wetlands during dry periods.

Most of Myakka's hammocks are treed with laurel oaks, live oaks, and sabal palms. Those adjacent to the river and lakes flood seasonally, though they are slightly higher in elevation than wetlands. Check out the tree trunks for water marks that reveal typical summer water levels. High water levels are also indicated by the line where lichens begin to grow on trees. Hammocks that flood usually have very little groundcover. Anything that grows low in these habitats must adapt to living in heavy shade and being covered by water for up to three months a year. Animals that call hammocks home include gray squirrels, gray foxes, barred owls, screech owls, cardinals, Carolina wrens, opossums, and raccoons. (You can read more about hammocks and swamps in Chapter 7, Shady Places.)

Sometimes people confuse shady, fire-excluded land with true hammocks. Over the four decades that the CCC and park staff endeavored to keep fire out of the park, oak trees invaded pine flatwoods and prairies. As the oaks formed a shaded overstory, palmettos grew taller in search of more light. As the grasses, herbs, and low shrubs shaded by increasingly dense palmettos began to die out, the animals that fed on these plants also died out or departed. You can find many examples of the result of Myakka's fire-excluded years. A canopy of oaks with a groundcover of high palmettos easily identifies them.

Now, how do you use this knowledge to read the land? The most obvious use is if you want to locate a particular type of animal. The best chance of finding it comes from visiting its preferred habitat. Biologists from the Florida Fish and Wildlife Conservation Commission used this method recently to locate sign of a Florida panther and document his presence with plaster casts of his tracks. Knowing panther habitat preferences enabled two trackers to locate sign in the far corners of the park within a few hours. They even got a bear track as a bonus that day.

When exploring cross-country, it is beneficial to be able to identify changes in communities from a distance. For instance, a ring of palmettos, wax myrtle, and gallberry taller than the surrounding vegetation usually indicates a marsh in the center. Large-crowned oaks seen from a distance often promise a thinner groundcover that will allow easier travel. An ecotone (the intersection of two habitats) is usually easier to travel and often contains more wildlife than the center of either community.

An understanding of what grows naturally can even help you find your way if you become lost. One day not long after the park assumed management of the Myakka Prairie, I went out on an all-terrain vehicle (ATV) to explore an unfamiliar area. The old road I was following traversed immense wetlands much deeper than I had expected. I meandered through an open hammock (not realizing I had lost the road), crossed an exceptionally deep wetland, and tried to locate signs of the road on the other side. I wandered into and out of hammocks and wetlands, detouring and taking another route each time I ran into overgrown prairie. Each wetland I negotiated seemed deeper than the last, and each time I found firm ground I took a deep breath, congratulated myself on making it through, and swore there was no way to return through that wetland without getting stuck! As the sun began to drop low in the sky I began to worry I wouldn't make it back before dark. Then I noticed something unusual about a medium-size wetland in front of me. A strip of tall broomsedge grass grew along the perimeter on one side of the marsh.

Broomsedge is relatively uncommon in undisturbed natural land. It grows most prolifically where the soil has been disturbed or the surrounding vegetation completely removed. Soil disturbance almost always indicates the effects of humans. So a symmetrical strip of solid broomsedge could mean only one thing—an old road. I followed the broomsedge around the marsh and into the prairie. Sure enough, the old road eventually ran into a more recently mowed road, and I was out of the woods long before sunset.

**Broomsedge**

# Adventure 1

## Old Friends and Their Relatives, Florally Speaking

**St. John's-wort**

Did you know that you can find a greater variety of plants in Florida than in almost any state in our country? And what a wonderful assortment we have! We have trees that start out as epiphytes—plants that derive moisture and nutrients from the air and rain and usually grow on other plants—and grow to devour full-grown palm trees; flowers so tiny you have to look through a microscope to see their miniature parts; and blossoms larger than your outstretched hand. We have carnivorous plants that thrive in poor soils by trapping and consuming insects. And there are even ferns that are not rooted in the ground but spend their entire lives growing on the branches of trees or floating in shallow ponds.

Myakka certainly has more than its share of diversity when it comes to plants. There are over 750 species on the park's plant list alone, and if you count the plants found throughout the Myakka

Island, the number is even higher. Becoming acquainted with even a portion of so many plants may seem formidable, but it can be easier than you'd imagine if you know an important secret.

Imagine attending a large party with over two hundred strangers. Your host introduces you to twenty of them. At the end of the evening, how many of those people's names would you remember? If you are like most people, you would remember three to five, especially if you found something interesting about those strangers.

But what if the twenty people you met were all related in some way to your closest friends? Say they were parents, brothers, sisters, or cousins of people you knew quite well. Perhaps you would notice something about each person that reminded you of your acquaintances—the same eyes or nose or body shape. You already know the last names of your friends, so if these people had the same last names you might remember the names of all twenty people. If you met them again a week later, you would probably still remember who they were or at least to which friend they were related. That's because you would associate them with a family name.

Plants also have families. Every single wildflower or tree belongs to a plant family. If you learn to identify the characteristics of a certain family, you can travel anywhere in the world, find an unfamiliar plant in that family, and immediately be familiar with a plant you have never seen before. The secret to learning how to identify plant families is to understand which characteristics are used to divide plants into families.

People often assume that plants with similar leaves are closely related. However, leaves are not a reliable indicator of plant relationships because plants are grouped into families by their flower parts. For instance, wild hibiscus flowers look very similar to hibiscus flowers in home landscapes. Some species of St. John's-wort have four petals and others have five, but the centers of the flowers all look remarkably alike because of the large number and arrangement of their stamens. Flowers in the milkweed family usually look as if they are growing upside down, and their leaves and stems have milky sap.

**Blueberry**

You are probably familiar with several plant families already. Many people can recognize members of the rose, pea, pine, and aster families by the shape of their flowers. Look closely at the flowers of plants you know and find out what families they belong to. As you learn to identify more plants and sort them into families, it will become easier to pick out the relatives of your old friends, both at Myakka and wherever you travel.

## Adventure 2

## How to Play in the Woods

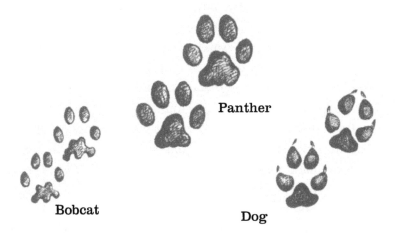

Panther

Bobcat

Dog

Having grown up in Florida during a time when almost every neighborhood had remnant patches of wild land that the local kids christened "the woods," I am often perplexed when park visitors ask if there is anything to do at the park when the airboat isn't running or the concession is closed.

In my childhood, even if the section of undeveloped woods was as small as a city block, it was large enough to hold mysteries ample enough to enchant a whole neighborhood of children summer after summer. Now when I play in the woods I draw upon my early experience with these mini-woods, and so can you. Though some childhood games have probably lost their appeal to older explorers of the woods, other wilderness pastimes can keep you entertained for hours. For instance, the youthful favorite, Building Forts, may not be enticing to adults, but other games—Animal Tracking and Survival, for example—are as fun as ever.

There are different phases of Animal Tracking. Finding animal tracks on dirt roads (especially after a summer shower) and matching the print to one identified on the pages of a field guide is good for the beginner. But the real fun comes when you follow tracks until they turn off into a shaded hammock or onto one of the hundreds of game trails that crisscross the woods. If you follow many game trails, you'll discover that animals, like people, have interstate highways, county roads, and country lanes. Our interstates connect major cities while our lanes lead only to the doorways of a few secluded houses. Likewise, game trails have specific purposes for wild creatures. Sometimes they lead to a sequestered water hole, sometimes to a blueberry patch. Each new trail begs you to discover its objective.

Lost in the Woods sounds dangerous on first thought. But if you go someplace where you are familiar with the boundaries, you'll realize the adventure in the game. There is an old railroad grade in Myakka that is called Powerline Road where it intersects with Park Drive. It crosses the park from the river (on the west) to the eastern park boundary. By examining the hiking trail map, you'll be confident that if you turn south off Powerline Road into the hammock, the section of land you're exploring is surrounded by a paved road to the west, a dirt road to the east, and a river to the south. So, no matter how many game trails you follow or how lost you get in the woods, you can always find your way out by heading towards a dependable boundary.

Survival is one of those private games you never admit to another adult that you play. It involves a fantasy like "I've been shipwrecked on a deserted island and now I must find food and shelter;" or "I'm living in Florida two hundred years ago and Indians are all around me." After you establish the requisite story line, you choose the best site for your shelter and plan what you would build it out of. Which plants are edible? What animal sign can you detect? You get the idea.

Mysteries of the Forest is not played in a single outing and may continue for years. At first it may be harder to find the questions than the answers. Often the riddles are so perplexing you persist in the quest to solve them long after you leave your wooded paradise. What makes the funny pyramids of mud at the edge of the marsh? Where do deer go in the heat of the day? What happens to the armadillos when the hammock floods? What do the mice eat after the woods burn?

Hidden Treasures is a game of chance. The treasures are the little surprises you come upon that you go home and tell your closest friend about—the intact set of antlers left by a buck deer; a shiny dung beetle attempting to roll a gigantic ball of scat (a woodsman's term for animal excrement) to some hopeless destination; a tiny secluded marsh covered with a yellow blanket of sunflower blooms.

Sounds of Discovery sharpens another of your senses. You never go into a wild place without hearing a new supply of mysterious sounds. One time I discovered that what seemed like a strange little bird calling was actually a leopard frog being swallowed by a blacksnake. I have amazed my friends by identifying the sound twice since.

As you play these games, you begin to advance to higher levels of skill. You begin to combine games, playing them simultaneously. Who made that hole in the ground? Who built that nest? Does this rubbing on the tree signify some creature's claim of territory? If so, can you find more to identify its range? What's that smell? What's in bloom? What's in fruit? What animal is close by? It's easy to catch the scent of a hog, and some woodsmen claim to be able to smell a deer hidden in a thicket.

What use are these games once you get really good at them? Well, it's a great way to spend an afternoon, and you'll certainly never again have to ask what there is to do in the park. But even more important is that the woods you explore become your own. And since it is human nature to defend one's own from outside threats, I hope a lot of people will claim Myakka as their own.

Hog

Raccoon

Turkey

Whitetail Deer

Opossum

Fox

Black Bear

Cotton Rat

Gray Squirrel

Animal tracks provided by Florida Fish and
Wildlife Conservation Commission

# Adventure 3

## Journey to Deer Prairie Slough

The trip to Deer Prairie Slough and back takes all day and should be undertaken only by those who have proven their stamina on shorter trips. I consider it the masterpiece of Myakka adventures, with rewards well worth the physical exertion invested. The journey begins with a 7.5-mile bicycle ride over dirt roads to the slough, includes a 2.5-mile hike around the edge of the slough, and ends with the return bicycle trip.

Begin at the intersection of North Park Drive and Fox's High Road. There's a chain across the dirt road but you can easily walk your bicycle around it. Ride down Fox's High Road and follow the map to Deer Prairie Slough. You will know you have reached the slough when you encounter the forested canopy. The route to Deer Prairie Slough is open and sunny and takes you through some of the best pine flatwoods and prairie habitat in the park. Take a few minutes to explore the diversity of the groundcover as you pass through Bee Island, especially on the north end of the pine stand. You may also want to take a break at Bee Island Campground. The campground is on Ranch House Road, just a few feet from where you will be passing down Bee Island Road. A splash of cool water from the pitcher pump is a welcome repose during a hot bicycle ride. Don't drink the water, however, unless you brought along some water purification tablets. Pitcher pumps can only lift water from shallow wells, so the water does not come from deep enough in the ground to be safe from bacteria.

When you reach the slough, leave your bicycle at the large clearing on the left where the rain gauge is installed. It is the site of the old rookery tower. Walk east on the railroad grade, over the bridge that

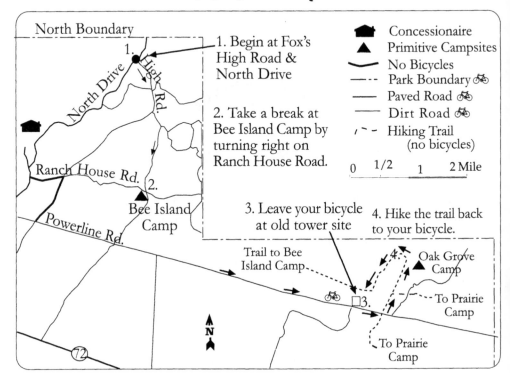

crosses the center of the slough, and then along the grade until you reach the hiking trail. You can recognize the trail by the small wooden footbridge on your left and the blue blaze marks on the trees along the trail. Cross the footbridge and follow the hiking trail north along the edge of the slough. It is a beautiful walk any time except during summer, when the trail floods, it is very hot, and there are scads of mosquitoes.

Stay on the main trail that follows the edge of the slough. Don't take the cutoff to Oak Grove or Prairie Camp. The trail will wind its way north to an old wooden bridge. After you cross the bridge, the trail turns south and follows the west edge of the slough. Follow the trail south until it takes an abrupt right turn and heads due west into the prairie. At that point you leave the hiking trail and just follow the slough edge, heading south until you reach the railroad grade. I usually pass right through the rain gauge clearing on my way to the road.

I always think of Deer Prairie Slough as the greenest place in the park. Ferns and epiphytes spread from treetop to ground level, and the bark of the trees is plastered with colorful lichens. The musky aroma of Myakka mud blends with the sweet scent of bay flowers, palmetto blossoms, or buttonbush blooms, and the sky is completely obscured by vines and treetops. The place just oozes wildness, like a jungle or a tropical rainforest.

When you pick your bicycle up at the old rookery tower site, you can return by the same route you traveled to reach the slough. Or, if the roads are not too sandy, you may want to choose another route from the map.

## Marsh Wade

**Pickerelweed**

The marsh wade is probably the most daring of the adventures described in this book. I remember my initiation to Myakka wetlands vividly. When Jean Huffman, the park biologist at the time, suggested I take off my shoes and socks to wade into the dark, murky water infested with snakes and alligators and bugs and who-knows-what-else, I was appalled. But as we waded slowly into the marsh, we began to pass through rings of vegetation. I could feel the changes in the soil beneath my bare feet as we moved from one plant zone into the next. As we moved out of the St. John's-wort into maidencane, then into arrowhead and finally pickerelweed, I could have identified the transition of plant species with my eyes closed just by the feel of the varying textures of mud beneath my toes. The longer I went without being eaten, bitten, or stung, the more comfortable I became in the wetland. She pointed out seedlings of St. John's-wort, which look totally different from the mature plant; green treefrogs on bulrush; swimming dragonfly nymphs; and feeding platforms built by marsh rats or round-tailed muskrats. The diversity was amazing.

I will always be grateful to Jean for introducing me to the world of wetlands. I have since indoctrinated hundreds of others. Now I usually wear tennis shoes when I lead a group of middle school or high school students thigh-deep into cool marsh water. We carry dip nets and hand lenses, traveling in single file past dragonflies laying eggs or camouflaged green treefrogs that think they can't be seen at all. We dip for minnows and tadpoles, and examine floating aquatic plants for their resident animal life.

"But what about the poisonous snakes and carnivorous alligators?" the teachers and parents want to know. Yes, they are out there, but we are not their prey. As long as you walk slowly, you give animals a chance to flee the area before you arrive. So I lead my small groups of students, all lined up behind me, to discover something they will remember all their lives. After all, who could ever forget a wade through a marsh?

You too can explore Myakka's wetlands. I think it's best to take a friend. Begin by exploring the outer zones of a shallow marsh. I would suggest those no more than knee-deep with maidencane edges. What I find so interesting about Myakka's wetlands is that each one seems totally different from the next. There are thousands to explore. Try walking into Big Flats Marsh along Park Drive, selecting an area that is not covered by the tall, thick, exotic paragrass. There are also several shallow marshes along Ranch House Road and along All Weather Road that are reasonably accessible.

Perhaps the best time to begin exploring wetlands is in the spring. Many of the isolated, seasonal ponds are dry that time of year, so you can examine the diversity of wetland plants and animals without even getting your feet wet. Alligators often claim their own wetlands during the dry season and keep the center excavated to hold water, so don't intrude into the deepest part of the marsh. I was surprised once to find that an alligator had dug a cave in the middle of a wetland I was exploring off of Ranch House Road. Instead of having to constantly wallow into a hole in the center, this gator just eased back into his cool, wet cave to await summer rains.

Note: *Florida Wetland Plants: An Identification Manual* is a great source for identifying wetland plants. You can purchase it from the Institute of Food and Agriculture Services at the University of Florida in Gainesville (800-226-1764). ⋌

drawn by H. McVay...

# 6

# Saving an Endangered Land— Florida Dry Prairie

A vast sea of grasses and wildflowers with isolated islands of slash pines and sabal palms once spanned between Orlando and Lake Okeechobee, stretching nearly from coast to coast. It was home to animals you'll now find scattered across the pages of endangered species lists, such as the Florida grasshopper sparrow, the burrowing owl, and the crested caracara. Today, only remnant patches of this rare community remain, making Florida dry prairie one of America's most endangered habitats.

Its imperiled state prompted the Florida Natural Areas Inventory (FNAI) to designate dry prairie as globally imperiled, ranking it right alongside the nation's rare Western tallgrass prairies. Richard Hilsonbeck, protection ecologist with the Nature Conservancy, once described our dry prairies as "Florida's most ignored and most imperiled natural resource."

Rarity is not the only characteristic shared by Florida prairies and those illustrious grasslands of the West. They share similar plants, animals, natural processes, intricate plant and animal interactions, and histories. The story's the same—only the names and places have been changed.

Let's begin our comparison of Western and Florida prairies by looking at their origins. Western prairies owe their existence to the Rocky Mountains. The mountain chain forms a barrier to passing weather systems that limits the amount of rainfall in the region. Scant rainfall means trees cannot survive. In more extreme conditions, a desert occurs.

Lightning created Florida's prairies. The region of the state where they occur has a higher frequency of lightning strikes than any other place in North America. For thousands of years, lightning-ignited fires swept across the prairies so frequently that all the plants and animals that lived there evolved to thrive with fire. It takes a lot of energy for plants to regrow after a fire passes through. And it's more efficient to produce underground growth parts that are protected by the cool earth than to produce primarily aboveground growth. The extensive root systems of prairies are often hundreds, maybe even thousands, of years old. That is why a large portion of plant growth will be found underground instead of aboveground, whether the prairie is in Oregon or Florida.

Western prairies also depend on fire. Without fire they begin to exchange their grassy/herbaceous groundcover for a shrubbier one, just as occurs in Florida prairies deprived of fire.

The similarity between prairie inhabitants, both plant and animal, in the East and in the West is quite interesting. Western grasses and wildflowers are often the same plants or near cousins of those growing in Florida prairies. Indian grass, little bluestem, and switchgrass (see species list appendix) are major grass components in tallgrass prairies. They grow among palmetto and wiregrass here. Rattlesnakemaster and butterflyweed grow in both places. Broomsedge, pinewoods dropseed, cordgrass, sumac, runner oak, asters, sunflowers, goldenrod, beardtongue, pine lilies, and blazing star growing in Florida prairies have sister species of the same genus out West.

Many of Florida's prairie animals are as imperiled as the land they call home. Some can be found nowhere else on earth. Could such unique fauna share any similarities with that of tallgrass prairies on the other side of the continent? Let's compare prairie denizens and their role in prairie ecology.

Bison and grasshoppers are the major plant consumers in Western tallgrass prairies. Here in Florida, white-tailed deer munch the herbage while thousands of grasshoppers spend their days catapulting from grass tips to flower petals. Out West, tallgrass prairie grasshoppers and other prairie insects are a major food source for many large birds such as sandpipers, meadowlarks, bobwhite quails, loggerhead shrikes, kestrels, and prairie chickens. At one time, swallow-tailed kites and long-billed curlews were part of this group. Florida prairie insects feed the same group of birds with the exception of prairie chickens. Sandhill cranes and snipe take their place, while swallow-tailed kites still circle overhead.

Western prairies harbor tiny grasslands birds, such as grasshopper and Henslow's sparrows, that weigh so little they can perch on and eat the seeds of the tall, swaying grasses without bending them to the ground. These grasslands birds also take advantage of the thick grass cover by nesting on or near the ground. Most of them have evolved to be able to renest if their first clutch of eggs is lost to predators or fire. Here in Florida, the federally endangered Florida grasshopper sparrow shares nesting areas with the little Bachman's sparrow, and the propensity to renest is a significant adaptation for birds in such fire-prone lands.

Tunnels of animals like Franklin's ground squirrel, badgers, and ants play an intricate role in Western prairie ecology. Not only does ground disturbance allow some prairie plants to compete that would otherwise not be able to get a foothold, but these tunnels also shelter Western prairie animals from heat and desiccating winds in summer and from the cold in winter. The gopher tortoise and burrowing owl dig into Florida prairies. Their homes afford protection from unrelenting summer sun for a long list of prairie animals. Over eighty different creatures may take refuge in burrows during a fire, and many of them call these burrows home.

Studying prairie plants and animals may shed light on merely a fraction of the entire prairie story. In their quest to enhance food crop production, soil scientists and biologists are looking under our natural areas and discovering a fascinating world of microscopic processes and intricate interdependencies that we would never have imagined. Some fungi form alliances with plants, in which the plants provide carbon to the fungi in exchange for assistance in taking up nutrients much more efficiently. The role of the tiny bacteria and other microscopic animals at the soil level in ensuring the health of the prairie is only beginning to be understood, and the discovery of mutually beneficial relationships of symbiotic plants and their co-hosts is revelatory.

Like Western prairies, Florida's grasslands have been almost ignored throughout Florida's history or valued only for what they could be transformed into rather than for any intrinsic value. Western prairies were converted into wheat fields and acres of corn as Florida prairies were consumed by tomato fields, citrus groves, pine plantations, and pastures of Bahiagrass. In fact, historical writings from early Florida residents and visitors seldom even mentioned the prairies. Writers considered them inhospitable, usually lumping them in with the impervious "wastelands" of the Everglades.

Only in the last couple of decades have people begun to pay attention to this once-vast community of south central Florida. Seldom studied and even less understood, the prairie remains an enigma to ecologists. In the past, many believed that prairies were simply clear-cut pine flatwoods or land burned so often by cattlemen that all the trees were killed off. Considering the similarities between prairies and flatwoods, it is easy to understand how these misconceptions originated. However, you have only to look at the early land surveys of the 1840s to discover that this was not the case. Later studies also revealed that some prairie animals are unable to exist in flatwoods and have always required prairies for sustenance.

Myakka's prairies were not understood or appreciated in earlier years. Surveyors charting the vast Myakka wilderness in the 1840s often judged the value of land by the timber it produced. They expressed their disdain for the grasslands by writing, "Perhaps it would be thought better had I surveyed more of the township's lines, however. This land in its entirety is so valueless that I did not warrant putting the government to further expense."

Not even the Florida Park Service understood the unique value of the prairie it managed. Early park rangers sat vigilant for the first wisp of smoke, always ready with fire flap, water tank, and fire plow. They planted row after row of pine trees in a misguided attempt to turn all that "wasteland" into productive forestland. Without fire the land began to change. Diminutive shrubs grew tall and acquired girth. Low-growing, slender palmetto stems took on gargantuan proportions, snaking along the prairie floor and then shooting up through the newly formed canopy of shrubs in competition for sunlight. First the myriad grasses and herbs that had been the foundation for this vivid ecosystem refused to flower; then more and more succumbed each year to the increasingly impenetrable mass of shrubs above them. Grasshopper sparrows, burrowing owls, caracaras, bobwhite quails, meadowlarks—one species after another disappeared as the habitat continued to deteriorate without fire.

It was in the 1980s that park management began to take aggressive action to restore the once-ubiquitous prairie. Park rangers had begun burning a decade earlier, but those early, infrequent, raging infernos set to back into winter winds bore little resemblance to the relatively quiet, meandering flames of natural lightning fires. First the rows of planted pines were removed. Then winter burns were replaced by growing season fires and the burn regime was increased to semiannually.

Park rangers watched anxiously for the transformation to begin. But something had happened to the woody plants of the prairie in all those years of fire exclusion. After each fire, palmettos and other shrubs quickly regrew to pre-fire stature, never giving grasses and herbs a chance to compete. That underground system of roots, the very mechanism that supported the prairie ecosystem, had been altered in some way. Instead of investing the effort to regrow above-ground plant mass every year or two when a fire passed through, the plants had put their energy into developing a root system to support their new structure of gargantuan shrubs. Since it is the root system that drives the prairie, once the new program had been initiated, it seemed as if it might be impossible to reprogram it back to its original function.

Areas most easily accessed by fire-suppression equipment over the decades were in the worst condition. In those areas, the number of plant species growing in a prairie that had once supported dozens had dwindled to only a handful. Sometimes all you could find there were shoulder-high palmetto, two or three species of head-high shrubs, and scattered sprigs of witch grass *(Dichantheleum sp)*. Prairies that were farther from the park shop or harder to get to were in better condition, still retaining a diversity of prairie plants.

That is when park staff began experimenting with low-intensity, restoration roller chopping. In those days, roller chopping was a controversial procedure, considered disastrous to natural areas by most environmentalists. Roller chopping had been used for years by ranchers to remove palmetto and establish "improved pasture" for cattle. But roller chopping administered by those land clearers involved the use of a huge, metal drum with spiked metal projections. The drum was filled with water to increase its weight and pulled behind a large tractor over the same area repeatedly. What if the drum were lighter and only made one pass across the land? Would the metal projections slice into the enlarged palmetto stems, stressing them without killing the entire plant? This would give any remaining herbaceous ground-cover a chance to compete.

A large section of moderately degraded prairie located several miles in the interior of the park was divided into plots, and a long-term experiment with restoration roller chopping began. Within just a few years, park staff could see the amazing results. Restoration roller chopping combined with frequent burning was restoring the original herbaceous composition of prairie in those areas that still contained a variety of prairie plants. By administering roller chopping in moderately degraded sections of prairie and gradually moving towards areas more seriously affected by fire exclusion, seeds of the original prairie inhabitants could be spread throughout the park.

Prairie restoration is expensive, time-consuming, and sometimes unpredictable. Roller chopping takes a toll on both equipment and people. Tractors are constantly in need of repairs after traveling over such rough terrain; tires are punctured often; and back problems plague tractor operators, requiring days of recuperation. Some years are too wet to burn, others so dry that bans on burning ruin carefully made burn plans. Each year park personnel must scramble to catch up from the most recent setback in burning or chopping.

But diligence has paid off. Every fall another new area is covered with wildflowers. Each year the populations of plants and animals once considered rare increase. As caracaras soar overhead, sparrows flitter from knee-high palmetto to thigh-high grass tops, and every step scares up a cluster of grasshoppers leaping in every direction, you can feel the richness of prairie life around you. And as you look into the distance and see where prairie meets sky, you can even imagine the grandeur of the great prairie that once stretched almost into infinity.

# Adventure 1

## Deciphering Myakka's Chop and Burn Checkerboard

If you look down on the plots from above, they resemble an asymmetrical checkerboard that looks as though it was fashioned haphazardly by a child's green crayon. You would never guess that these mysterious, irregular blocks of land hold the secret to restoring Myakka's upland communities.

It all seemed so naively simple back in the mid-1980s: restore frequent fire to the prairies and pinelands, then watch the transformation back into the colorful grasslands they had been prior to fire exclusion. But after nearly a decade of conscientious burning, frustrated park personnel began to realize that physiological changes had occurred in the palmettos and other shrubs after so many years without fire. The long-awaited reduction of shrubs and increase in grasses and wildflowers were not materializing as expected.

In 1987, researchers from the University of Florida designed a study to compare two different kinds of land management treatments: roller chopping and burning. They sectioned an area between the power line and S. R. 72 into a grid of six- to fifteen-acre plots. Two plots were chopped, one in January and one in June. This treatment was repeated every six years. Two other plots were burned at three-year intervals, one plot in January and one in June. Plots in the third group were chopped once, and then burned every three years (one plot with winter burns, the other with summer burns).

The results were so enlightening that park management began to use these techniques on a larger scale throughout the park. Myakka River has been so successful with the pioneering technique of low-

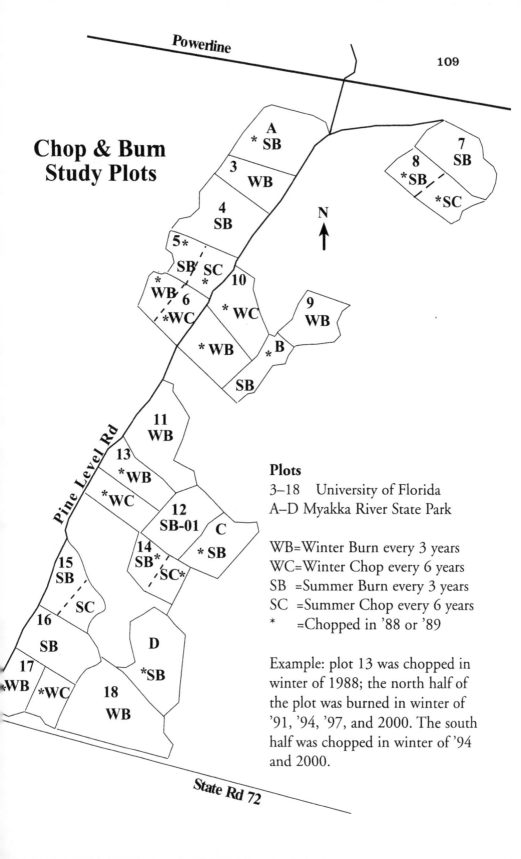

# Chop & Burn
# Study Plots

Powerline

A
* SB

3
WB

4
SB

5 *
SB' SC

*
WB 6
*WC

*

10

* WC

9
WB

* WB

* B

SB

7
SB

8
*SB

*SC

N
↑

11
WB

13
*WB

*WC

12
SB-01

C

14
SB*

SC*

* SB

15
SB

SC

16

SB

D

17

WB

*WC

18

WB

*SB

Pine Level Rd

State Rd 72

**Plots**
3–18    University of Florida
A–D Myakka River State Park

WB=Winter Burn every 3 years
WC=Winter Chop every 6 years
SB =Summer Burn every 3 years
SC =Summer Chop every 6 years
*      =Chopped in '88 or '89

Example: plot 13 was chopped in winter of 1988; the north half of the plot was burned in winter of '91, '94, '97, and 2000. The south half was chopped in winter of '94 and 2000.

impact roller chopping followed by frequent fire that land managers throughout the Southeast are beginning to duplicate these methods for uplands restoration in other natural areas. Over the years we have learned that what works best in Myakka prairies is a single chop followed by growing-season burns every two years.

The study plots were chopped and burned to prescription for fifteen years. The study was discontinued in 2005 and the entire area put on a two-to-three-year burn rotation. The map indicates the treatment program for each plot. You can visit the area by hiking or biking. If you go on bicycle, you may have to walk through areas that are plowed up by hogs, seasonally flooded, or tilled for firelines. Be sure to take a compass, as it is easy to get disoriented in the grid.

My favorite time to visit the study plots is in the fall, when explosions of flowering grasses and wildflowers signify success in various plots. Your chances of finding the best blooms depend on how wet or dry the year has been and how recently the area burned. Plots that have not burned in three years seldom put forth as many blossoms as those that have been burned during the past one or two years. Pine lilies bloom from mid-September to mid-October; blazing stars and the *Carphephoruses* (wild vanilla, deer tongue, Florida paintbrush) come next in September or October; the goldenasters and sunflowers bloom around mid to late October. You can find meadow beauties, marsh pinks, bachelor's buttons, and yellow-eyed grass nearly year-round.

## Adventure 2

# Hunting for Pine Lilies in Autumn

**Pine lily**

Old-time Floridians called them tiger or leopard lilies. The brilliant, red-orange blossoms dotted the prairies and flatwoods in September and October and were so impressive that they endured as lifelong memories for anyone who roamed the wild lands of Florida.

At Myakka River State Park, the pine lily has become the symbol of success in the quest to return prairies to the sunny grasslands described by travelers to Florida more than a century ago. As researchers at the park searched for the best tools and methods to restore the prairie, they found that most studies focused on measuring changes in major plant species like palmetto and wiregrass. But what is happening to those plants that are not so common? the park biologist at that time wanted to know. How can we judge the impact of fire season and roller chopping on less common plants? What if our management techniques are accomplishing the desired effect of reducing shrubs while increasing herbs and grasses but are eliminating plants that occur less frequently?

In 1988, a study was designed to track the response of pine lilies to various management treatments. The pine lily was chosen because its brightly colored flowers are easy to pick out among palmettos and grasses. Each week throughout September and October, researchers and volunteers would zigzag across study plots, counting and recording the number of lilies that bloomed.

Pine lilies don't bloom in overgrown prairies deprived of fire. Though lilies have the ability to lie dormant for many years awaiting the return of fire, if shrubs get too thick or high, the flowers refuse to bloom. As Myakka's land managers determined the effects of various management treatments on a minor plant species, they began to recognize the lily bloom as an indicator of a healthy prairie.

So every September I anxiously survey the roadsides and prairie edges for the year's first pine lily. It's a bit like waiting for your report card or an editor's comments on your most recent piece of writing. How has nature judged our management efforts this year? Where will the most colorful autumn blooms appear? Of course, nature does have some input into the equation. No matter how much rangers chop or burn, an extremely wet or dry July and August reduce the number of orange and yellow heads popping up over the surrounding grasses and palmettos. One year the winter was very wet, followed by an extremely dry spring and a moderately wet summer. The pine lilies, deer tongue, wild vanilla, and goldenasters were everywhere. I danced in the prairies in sheer exhilaration that fall with each new patch of fall blooms I discovered.

If you get an opportunity to visit the park from mid-September through mid-October, take time out to go pine-lily hunting. Ask at the Ranger Station where the flowers have been seen recently. The less time you spend looking for the best blooms, the more time you can spend enjoying them.

Areas of the park that have been blessed with the most abundant lily blooms in the past include the chop-and-burn study plots, Bee Island Road, All Weather Road, the east portion of Ranch House Road, and South Powerline Road. ⚘

# 7

# Shady Places— Swamps and Hammocks

Myakka is a land shaped by fire, and its shady places are just as dependent on their relationship with this natural phenomenon as the pinelands and prairies. The difference is that the pinelands and prairies developed because they were frequently burned by fire while the swamps and hammocks developed because they were protected in some way from fire over the centuries.

Southern breezes are the prevalent winds during the time of year we are most likely to have lightning fires. On a typical late spring or summer day, a thunderstorm moves in. Lightning preceding the storm strikes a pine tree or clump of grass and ignites a small fire. Winds are erratic with the approaching thunderhead, and the fire burns in varying directions. If rain follows, the fire is put out. If not, the wind usually returns to its original course and the fire rambles on to the north, northeast, or northwest.

If the fire encounters a dry, shallow, grassy wetland, the marsh

will burn. But if the wetland is deeper and covered with water or succulent vegetation, the fire burns around the pond, then continues its
route, sparing the northern perimeter of the marsh. As this pattern
repeats itself for hundreds of years, areas protected from fire support
trees and other plants that have not adapted to frequent fire, thus
becoming hammocks or swamps. If you examine a map of Myakka's
natural communities, you will see that the true hammocks often lie on
the north side of large, deep, or permanent wetlands.

From about mid-October until late June or July, most park visitors consider Myakka's shady places the most inviting habitats in the
park. The shady canopy shields them from the sun and the forest floor
is relatively clear of vegetation, making exploration easier than in any
of the other communities. But most plants and animals don't share
this attraction to shady places. There are fewer species of plants and
animals living in hammocks and swamps than in any of Myakka's
other natural areas. Why don't other species find hammocks as inviting as we do?

First of all, any plant that grows there must be adapted to heavy
shade. Flowering plants usually depend on the sun's rays to flower and
seed. Few are able to carry out that process in low-light situations.
Those that are most successful are the ones that can somehow find
sunlight—trees that send branches up through the canopy, vines that
continue to grow upward, or epiphytes that grow high in the treetops.

The next problem is flooding. Myakka's hammocks and swamps
may be inundated with water throughout the entire summer. Few
low-growing plants on a forest floor can survive being covered with
water for months at a time. Then they must still be able to survive the
long dry season without water. Perhaps one reason there are fewer
plants on the forest floor in Myakka's hammocks than in its swamps is
that hammocks are dry much longer than swamps.

Animals living in these forested areas must be able to climb or fly
to escape the rising waters and to reach seeds and fruits high in the forest canopy. Animals that prey upon the plant eaters need to be able to
reach their prey or be large enough to move into and out of the flood-

ed forest with its seasonal changes. So in some ways the habitats that are most inviting to humans may seem as severe as deserts to other organisms: they're too wet, too dry, or too shady too much of the year.

Swamps are forested wetlands that stay wet long enough to sustain wetland plants like maple, black gum, cypress, Carolina ash (pop ash), willow, royal fern, swamp fern, canna lily, lizard's tail, and golden club. Myakka's swamps range from tiny depressions filled with multi-trunked pop ash surrounded by hammock (found along Park Drive) to the impressive forested wetland that crosses through the eastern portion of the park known as Deer Prairie Slough. (A slough is a chain of connected wetlands in which water flows toward a river, lake, or bay during the wet season.) Deer Prairie Slough is probably the most diverse of Myakka's shady places, which makes it very interesting to explore during the driest times of the year.

A bayhead, or baygall, is a forested wetland that is dominated by bay trees. The name "bay" is a common name used for four species of trees that often grow together but that actually belong in three different families. Loblolly bay is in the tea family; silver bay is actually a magnolia; and red bay and swamp bay are in the laurel family. When viewed from a distance, these wetlands seem to form a dome with the trees in the center a bit taller than those around the edges. The ground is often covered with ferns and tangled vines. There is a good example of a bayhead on the hiking trail just before you reach Bee Island Camp.

It is Myakka's hammocks that have become the focus of attention since the construction of the canopy walkway early in 2000. Ecological processes that were previously taken for granted are now being scrutinized to better define their mechanisms and function. For instance, we understand that epiphytic tank bromeliads, once common in Myakka's forest canopy, catch water in their rosette of leaves, enabling them to thrive under dry conditions. It is also well known that insects, reptiles, and amphibians visit these miniature pools to quench their thirst. But how many creatures are actually dependent on these handy water sources and would not be able to exist without them?

Answering that question may soon be more practical than anyone could have imagined just a few years ago. If the invading Mexican weevil (accidentally released into south Florida's natural areas around 1990) continues to decimate the large bromeliads, creatures entirely dependent upon pineapple and cardinal airplants will also disappear. If some of the airplant visitors are responsible for pollinating palm trees, other plants in the hammock ecosystem, or plants in adjoining habitats, what decreases in fruit production will follow? What plants will be eliminated entirely? What other links in the chain will be lost? How much do migrating warblers rely on Myakka's hammock canopies? Do they drink from large airplants or feed on bromeliad residents?

Canopy science is still a pioneer field for scientific study, and ecologists are frantically studying the treetops of our planet's most productive forests in hopes of gleaning their secrets before they disappear. But the canopy of a tropical rainforest is so complex that it is often difficult to link all of its many intricacies. What if scientists could study a similar but simpler version and apply what they learn to the more complex rainforest ecosystem? Canopy scientists in Sarasota are looking to Myakka's subtropical treetops with just that possibility in mind.

As these researchers delve into the mysteries of forest canopy life at Myakka, they expect to also discover Myakka-specific data that will provide insight into the Myakka ecosystem. The park lacks any kind of comprehensive lists of insects. We have no information on the types of lichens found here. We don't even know the identities of the myriad pollinators that flock around a sabal palm when it is in bloom. Flying squirrels are noted on our list of resident vertebrate species, but how abundant are they and where in the park can they be found? What happens to ground-burrowing animals like shrews or other small mammals when the hammocks flood? Do they become itinerant canopy residents? There is so much we still don't know, and there are still many questions we have not yet thought to ask.

## Adventure 1

# In Search of Myakka's Baby Snooks

This adventure begins with a story, then sends you on a mission to search for artifacts from the time when the park was new. The story was told to me by Joe Crowley, the son of one of Myakka's first park managers, Allen Crowley.

Allen Crowley grew up in Old Miakka just a few miles from the north boundary of what is now Myakka River State Park. In his young life he had witnessed the demise of game animals in the region. It began before the turn of the century as the Myakka valley became world famous for hunting opportunities. Then, when the Depression arrived, most people looked to the wilds to put food on their tables. By the time the park was established in 1941, there were no turkeys or deer anywhere in Sarasota or its adjoining counties, according to residents of that era.

When Allen landed the job as park superintendent at one of Florida's first state parks, his dream was to reestablish turkey and deer. In those days the job was neither lucrative nor prestigious, but for the Old Miakka native it became a lifelong passion. Joe said Allen declined a job offer from the Palmer Ranch (with three times the pay) to work at the park. As park superintendent, Allen was on duty or on call seven days a week around the clock, according to Joe.

The game warden back in those days was Lefty Taylor. One day, Allen heard that Lefty's brother, who was living in the Everglades, had some live turkeys for sale. Allen got into his beat-up, old station wagon and drove all the way down to the Everglades to purchase two hen turkeys and a gobbler. He paid $15 apiece for the birds. There was no park budget back then, so he purchased them with his own funds—quite an expenditure since his salary was only $76 per month.

Park staff built a huge pen of field wire off what we now call Ranch House Road. (Joe called it Deer Pen Road, as do some of the older park rangers I have interviewed.) The fence was about eight feet high and surrounded six acres. Park neighbors donated the materials. Crowley put the turkeys into the pen to breed.

One day Allen received a call from Lefty's brother. An orphaned fawn was in need of someone to care for it. Was Allen interested in taking on the task? Allen got into his old car and again made the long drive down to pick up the little deer. Back at Myakka, the fawn was bottle-fed and cared for until she was strong enough to make the rounds in the campground. She soon learned to take advantage of her status as the only deer in town, going from campsite to campsite for handouts and attention. Named Baby Snooks after a popular radio star of the day, the fawn became the darling of park visitors and nearby residents. She would often catch the school bus with the local children, and the bus driver would have to call to have someone pick her up at the school in town.

When the classic movie *The Yearling* was filmed in Florida in 1946, the producer obtained the animals needed for the movie from Bonita Springs Animal Gardens. But Bonita Springs didn't have a fawn. "Go talk to Allen Crowley over at the Myakka Park," the owner told the producer. And he did. And that's how the fawn of Baby Snooks came to star in a movie.

Crowley purchased three more deer at Bonita Springs Animal Gardens, again with his own funds. He brought home one buck and two does and put them into the six-acre pen. Each year he released the does' fawns into the park. (Each doe had twin fawns, which Joe thought was quite unusual.) Soon there were about thirty-five deer grazing on Big Flats Marsh.

It's been over half a century since Allen Crowley embarked on his crusade to restock Myakka with turkey and deer. Now each spring it's a common sight to see proud mother hen turkeys herding long strings of chicks across Park Drive. You can go out almost any evening or early morning and spot deer grazing along the road shoulder. And every now and then an elderly park visitor asks, "Whatever happened to Baby Snooks?"

"Oh, she's still out there, all right," I reply. "Just go out to Big Flats Marsh just after sunset. If you look very carefully, you can still find her in the descendents she left behind."

You can still find remnants of the six-acre fenced compound that produced such an abundance of wildlife. Walk down Ranch House Road (from Park Drive) to a small marsh on the right (south) side of the road. Turn into the woods and follow the east edge of the marsh (about a hundred yards) until you reach the palmetto line. If you head east into the hammock at that point and follow a small creek that leads to a game trail that cuts through a small patch of tall palmetto, you'll

**Audrey Mead and Baby Snooks, 1947**

find parts of the old fence line in the clearing ahead. There are also silo foundations just southeast of the old fence line. Read the next adventure to discover their story. You can also find fence remnants by walking along Ranch House Road until you pass the site of the old ranch house. There is a fence close to the road that many people think is a relic from ranch house days, but now you know the truth.

"This is your park. I'm the only one here and I can't do it all, so I need your help," Allen would tell park visitors. The community rallied around the dedicated park superintendent. If he needed anything, all he had to do was pick up a phone and someone would come running. The community understood his quiet dedication and appreciated his efforts (and success) in bringing deer and turkey back to Myakka River. When Allen died in 1972, the Audubon Society erected a small stone monument in his memory at the birdwalk, which had been one of his favorite achievements during his long career at Myakka River State Park.

# Bertha Palmer's Meadowsweet Pastures and Frank Tucker's Tree House

### Bertha Palmer's Meadowsweet Pastures

When Bertha Palmer came to town, the fate of Sarasota was changed forever. Almost overnight, the little fishing village was put on the map. Her land purchases and other investments boosted the town's economy to an unprecedented high. One man I interviewed told me it seemed as though half the town was on her payroll, participating in one or another of her various enterprises. Though she had married one of Chicago's richest men, she was never obscured by his shadow, and she certainly made a name and a fortune for herself after his death. Stories abound about the life and times of Mrs. Potter Honore Palmer, and many of them can be discovered at a historical site south of Sarasota called Spanish Point at the Oaks, the location of her Florida home. But the story that is of interest to us here is how she came to own a large part of what is now Myakka River State Park.

One day, after she had bought up all the best land Sarasota had to offer, Arthur Edwards brought her all the way out to Myakka in his horse-drawn buggy to a ridge along Vanderipe Slough that overlooked the Myakka River. She declared the spot to be the most beautiful of all and asked how much it would cost to buy it. When Edwards told her it was part of a cattle ranch owned by Dink Murphy, she declared that if he would sell her the ranch, she would buy his cattle too. An agreement was reached and she promptly wrote out a check for $93,000 for the six-thousand-acre ranch. That was how Bertha Palmer became a rancher.

She named her ranch Meadowsweet Pastures and, at age sixty-one, pursued her new career with the same fervor as she had invested in her many past endeavors. Bertha Palmer is credited with changing forever the way cattle ranches were run in Florida. She fenced her ranch when all of Florida was still open range. She built dip tanks to dip her cattle for the ticks that plagued them. (She was ridiculed for her efforts during her lifetime, but after her death it became mandatory in Florida that all cattle be dipped.) She imported Brahma bulls to improve her Florida scrub cow herd. The experiment was immensely successful, and soon ranchers all over the state were using the breed. But her brief ranch career ended with her death in 1918, only eight years after she arrived in Sarasota. Thanks to the inspiration of and prompting by Arthur Edwards, Bertha's sons donated nineteen hundred acres of her land, the first piece of property acquired for Myakka River State Park.

Bertha Palmer never lived at her ranch in Myakka, though she visited it often. She hired a foreman to live at and run the enterprise. I interviewed Walt Sweeting, the son of Meadowsweet Pastures' second ranch foreman, Eugene Sweeting. Walt lived on the ranch for a dozen years or so as a young boy and teenager. As we walked through the hammock south of Ranch House Road, he described the ranch and what he remembered about life at the ranch.

When Mrs. Palmer wanted to "rough it," she would camp at the area that you find the concession today. Concrete pillars were built about three feet high, with a round platform of cypress connecting them. There were several of these structures. Tent poles were put on the concrete pillars and the tents spread over the cypress floor. A long, cypress building was constructed for cooking. Both the ranch house and the lake area were extensively lit by bright, electric lights (unheard of in the wilds of Myakka in those days), powered by a Delco generator plant. It was the ranch foreman's job to keep the large batteries full of water and in good condition. "You'd be standing down at the lake and slowly the lights would start to dim. Then all of a sudden the lights would flash bright and you'd know the Delco plant was cutting back on," Walt reminisced.

The ranch house was a two-story, wooden structure with a screened porch around the entire second story (screen was also a luxury in those days). I also interviewed Walt's sister, Florabelle, who recalled watching the train pass along the railroad tracks from her upstairs bedroom window. If you visit the ranch house site, look to the south through the forest of oaks and imagine how much the area has changed since Florabelle watched those trains through her window.

An artesian well at the back of the house supplied the family with water (without electricity or any other type of power to pump it) except in the driest parts of the year. (The well was still working when I began to work at the park. You just had to turn the valve and the water flowed out.) Just north of the house was a huge water tank standing on concrete pillars. The water tank held rainwater for those times when the water table was so low that the artesian well was not producing. The tank was often used by the children and the ranch hands to shower. The concrete foundation blocks are still visible as you travel along Ranch House Road. Many people mistakenly believe that they are the ranch house foundation blocks.

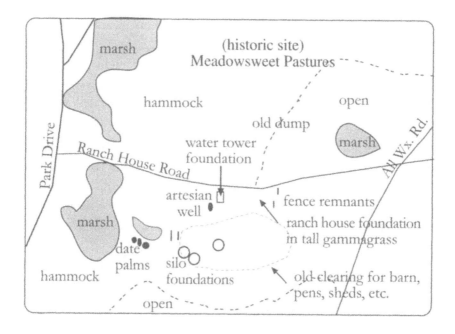

There were three circular, concrete structures southwest of the house. Two of them were silo foundations. Walt said they were built for storing food for Black Angus cows (which turned out to be too fragile to endure the flies and rigors of Florida ranch life). The third structure was a compost bin, according to Walt. He said the children found the concrete enclosure perfect for keeping baby alligators as pets. There were also a barn, a slaughterhouse, a blacksmith shop, a goat pen, and enclosures for horses and mules.

Few trees grew on the ranch. Oaks and palms grew between the house and Upper Lake, and pine trees grew at Bee Island. At that time the pine island was larger, with about two hundred acres of huge, beautiful longleaf pines. The rest of the ranch was prairie with two-foot-high palmetto, lots of grasses, daisies, and tiger lilies. Very often the wiregrass was taller than the palmetto.

Vultures were even more numerous then than they are today.

According to Walt, there were ten times as many. When a cow died, there would be at least two hundred buzzards on it, and there were also quite a few "Mexican buzzards" (caracaras).

Walt said the ranch hands sometimes killed eight or ten rattlesnakes a day while working the cattle. He recalled riding with Dink Murphy on a cattle round-up when he was a young boy. Mr. Murphy always carried a long bullwhip, so heavy that Walt could barely pick it up, let alone get it to crack. When the cattle began to move, the snakes would feel the vibration and start to move too. Every once in a while, one would stick its head up out of the palmetto to look around and Dink would pop his whip at it. Walt would keep an eye on the spot, and when he arrived he'd look around, hoping to prove a miss. Every time he'd find a rattlesnake with its head snapped off.

The area where the two-story ranch house once stood is south of Ranch House Road, east of Park Drive. It is the same area where Allen Crowley built the five-acre pen to hold his deer and turkeys. If you find any remnants of ranch house days, just leave them where you find them. The park service may someday decide to do an archeological study of the area.

## Frank Tucker's Tree House

In the 1930s, Frank Tucker owned the land that is now the boat basin at Myakka River State Park. As a Sarasota native, he was quite familiar with the ways of the river, so when he wanted to build his "weekend get-away cottage" there, he built two tree houses instead of a conventional cabin. Many longtime park visitors remember the tree houses and stop to ask about their fate. Having heard about them for so many years, I was pleased when I got the chance to speak to Frank Tucker's daughter, Eula Tucker Lastinger, a few years back. She told me all about the tree houses:

> There were two of them. One was a two-bedroom. The rooms were just large enough for a bed and a dresser. The other one was a one-bedroom and the downstairs was on the ground.

We had our living quarters there; in other words it was the bedrooms that were up in the tree. It was all screen except one end of it and that was walled up like you find in an efficiency apartment. That was covered over so we could lock things up in there when we left. There was a stove and a little icebox that you put ice in. We kept a few groceries out there. We just had a ladder to get up to the tree house. The tree house was very substantially built. You realize that we didn't have the drainage that we have today. I suppose that is the reason that people didn't have houses out there.

When the land was acquired for the park, the state used the eminent domain law to acquire the Tucker property and tree houses. The tree houses were moved down to where the river gauge is today, behind the log picnic area. That was also the site of the first concession. I've also heard that the state rented the tree houses out to visitors and that an early park ranger lived in one of them.

photo provided by Eula Tucker Lastinger

## Adventure 3

## A Walk Through the Treetops

The Myakka canopy walkway was the inspiration of canopy scientist Margaret Lowman. After spending a couple of decades devising methods to study treetops in the forests of other continents, Dr. Lowman settled in as the director of Sarasota's Marie Selby Botanical Gardens. Though her experience was with tropical ecosystems, she realized that

Florida's forests were as imperiled as many of the legendary rainforests. Why not use the same methods employed to study and conserve the canopies of faraway endangered forests to save our own threatened ecosystems?

Little research exists on the canopies of subtropical forests. Dr. Lowman's position provided an opportunity to augment current knowledge. She began studying Myakka's treetops with traditional methods that included ropes, ladders, and pulleys. Then she devised a plan to build a walkway through the treetops, as had been done at several of her previous research stations. By building a canopy walkway at a popular state park, she could not only carry out Selby's research objectives but also entrance the general public with her passion: conserving our planet's forests.

Dr. Lowman had yet a third agenda for her planned walkway. While raising her two sons, she had seen the declining interest of students in the sciences. If teachers could involve their students in actual research projects at the walkway, not only would valuable data be gained, but perhaps the experience could forever change the way the students perceived the sciences and their natural world.

A partnership among Selby Gardens, Friends of the Myakka River, and the state park, combined with the generous support of local grant foundations, businesses, and area residents, resulted in an eighty-five-foot-long suspended bridge through the treetops and a seventy-four-foot tower. The structure was opened to

**Mexican weevil**

the public in June 2000 and was an instant hit with park visitors. It's easy to see why. You can look down onto bromeliad airplants perched high in the oaks, come within a few feet of the blossoms of butterfly orchids, compare the colorful lichens growing high in the trees with those closer to the ground, and peruse the branches for arboreal insects like leaf hoppers and noisy cicadas. From the tower you can see the Upper and Lower Myakka Lakes, the serpentine river, a patchwork of shades of green that distinguishes one tree species from another, and the abrupt end of the tree line as the hammock meets the flat prairie. You can look down on raptors soaring beneath you, a strange perspective for identifying hawks, eagles, and kites. And from that vantage point you can almost imagine that you are deep in a vast wilderness devoid of human development (if you ignore the occasional rooftop that pops up along the park's western border).

The walkway proved its practical value with a shocking discovery a few months after it opened. An exotic weevil from Central America that had accidentally been released in the Ft. Lauderdale area in the early 1990s had made its way to the treetops of Myakka River. The weevil infests and devours the hearts of large epiphytes like the pineapple and cardinal airplants found in Myakka's trees. Wherever the insect invades, the airplants are decimated and eventually eliminated from the patch of forest. The bugs travel from treetop to treetop and will likely infest all the large bromeliads in the entire state if a remedy is not devised.

By early 2001, the weevil was widespread throughout the park. Pineapple airplants and cardinal airplants had been designated endangered species. Though no remedy has been perfected to destroy the weevil, valuable information has been gleaned from research that increases the possibility of saving these keystone hammock species.

The Mexican evil weevil and its host bromeliads became the first study subjects at the canopy walkway. Schoolchildren learned about the vital role epiphytes play in hammock ecology and then came out to count airplants infested by the weevil. College students initiated inventory projects in specific areas of the park. Researchers from the University of Florida studying the life cycle of the destructive bug devised a plan to make Myakka one of the first test sites to release a fly as a biological control. Though much research needs to be done before the fly can be released (to ensure that the fly preys only on the Mexican weevil), the project gives us hope for the future.

The canopy walkway is located on a spur trail off the Boylston Nature Trail about a mile from S.R. 72. It is open the same hours as the park and is available to campers any time of day or night. During the season, park volunteers are at the walkway at peak visitation times to answer questions and point out some of the interesting features of the hammock.

*Note: Visit the Florida Council of Bromeliad Societies web site at http://fcbs.org/ to learn more about the weevil and discover what you can do to help.

# Adventure 4

# The High Road to Fox's Loop Trail

This ninety-minute hike is about one-third sunny and two-thirds shady. It begins at Fox's High Road, the service road closest to the north gate, just south of Clay Gully Bridge. Read Chapter 4, Fire, Most Naturally, for a better perspective on the area. Then follow the map shown here.

You should encounter wildflowers along the sunny service roads, find epiphytes in the hammock along the trail, experience the difference between true hammock and fire-excluded prairie edge, and hear a nice assortment of frog- and birdcalls to identify. If you hike during the summer, expect to get your feet wet. The hammock usually floods after the summer rains begin. If it's a warm day, you can start early in the sunny part of the walk and spend the rest of your hike in the shade.

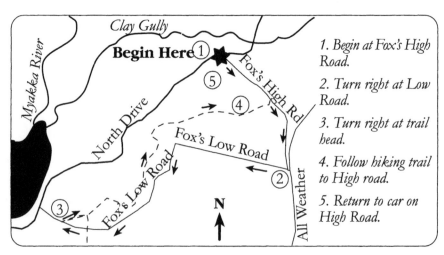

1. Begin at Fox's High Road.

2. Turn right at Low Road.

3. Turn right at trail head.

4. Follow hiking trail to High road.

5. Return to car on High Road.

# Adventure 5

## Looking for Lichens

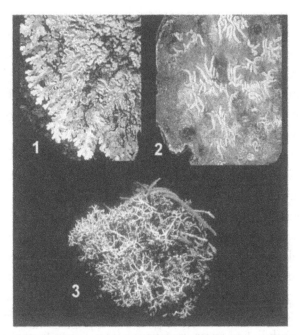

1. foliose lichen 2. crustose lichen 3. fruticose lichen

Animal, Vegetable, or Mineral? Did you ever play that childhood game? In my youth, all of nature's components were believed to fit neatly into one of those categories—the three kingdoms. But this adventure is going to send you in pursuit of something so mysterious that scientists had to come up with an entirely new kingdom in which to place it. Unless your dictionary is brand new, it probably says that a lichen is a plant. It is not. It may say that a lichen is an organism with two components that form a symbiotic relationship. Wrong again, because it is not an organism. It is a group of organisms. And those organisms do not even belong to the same kingdom.

These days, ecologists usually divide all living things into five kingdoms: plants, animals, fungi, algae, and bacteria. The modern approach to lichens is to look at them as mini-ecosystems. These tiny ecosystems consist of at least one fungus and either a green alga or a cyanobacterium that merge together to make up a life form that can thrive in the driest deserts; in the coldest, most inhospitable regions; or even where no other life can exist. The organisms that bond to form a lichen may be from as many as three different kingdoms, and each of the partners gains benefits by the association. The name we give each lichen refers to its fungal partner because each lichen has a unique fungus. That is why lichens are classified in the fungi kingdom. Algae and cyanobacteria, most of which occur in many different lichens, have their own names.

Most algae and bacteria that form lichens can live only in aquatic or very wet, terrestrial habitats. But embedded in fungi to form lichens, they can exist in very dry conditions. The fungi supply the algae or bacteria with water and minerals and shelters them to prevent them from drying out. However, it is the fungi that gain the most from the relationship. When living as individuals, fungi are not capable of producing food. They must get their nutrients parasitically from a host or from decaying plant or animal life. Algae and cyanobacteria contain chlorophyll, which enables fungi to manufacture the food supply for both lichen partners. Cyanobacteria even have the ability to capture and fix nitrogen from the atmosphere.

Myakka grows a wide assortment of some very beautiful lichens. Since no one has ever inventoried Myakka's lichens, I can't even guess how many there may be. My favorite Myakka Christmas was spent in the field with a couple of visiting lichen experts who had one day to photograph as many of Myakka's lichens as they could find for a book entitled *Lichens of North America* (Yale University Press, 2001). (At www.lichen.com there is an excellent website that features beautiful photographs, a list of the ways lichens have been used by people, and a large helping of lichen information.) I took this opportunity to begin a collection for the park. In a few hours we brought back sixteen different species that could be identified (at least to genus level).

Begin your lichen expedition by examining laurel oaks, maples, and bay trees in picnic areas and along shady roads like Ranch House Road. Then branch out to other types of habitats to find a greater diversity of lichens. You can compare those in the treetops to those you find at ground level by visiting the canopy walkway. Compare the ones you find in wet areas to those you find in more xeric (dry) conditions. (Note: A ten-power magnifying lens will definitely enhance your lichen-hunting experience. Ten-power lenses are available for sale at the Ranger Station.)

A lichen is usually categorized into one of three different growth forms: crustose, foliose, or fruticose. You can find examples of each kind in Myakka. Crustose (crusty) lichens grow crustlike on tree bark. (They also grow on rocks in other regions.) An assortment of crustose lichens looks as if someone painted a wild canvas by blotching it with various colors of paint. The pink and white splotches on the trees in the oak hammocks are examples of crustose lichens.

Foliose (leaflike) lichens are attached only in spots. Their outside edges are lobed and are not attached to the tree. The pale, grayish-green shield lichen is a type of foliose lichen. It looks kind of like fancy lace growing along the small branches of trees, particularly dead branches. Some lichens derive some of their nutrition parasitically from mosses or decaying wood and bark.

The third growth form is fruticose (shrubby) lichens, which are branched, upright, or hanging plants. Beard lichen looks like dainty hairpin lace with tiny tatted circles. It hangs down about two inches from the smaller branches of hardwoods. Deer moss grows in sandy, scrub areas. It's the little two- to three-inch balls of pale green that are often used in model train landscapes to form the shrubbery.

Lichens are often the first life forms to enter an area barren of plant life, colonizing on bare soil and rocks to prepare the soil for plant life. On nutrient-poor soils, lichens accumulate and release nutrients required by forest trees for growth. They can even survive in the freshwater streams of saltwater tidal zones. In the Arctic and Antarctic, lichens are sometimes the only source of food for reindeer and caribou and are eaten by the people of those regions when other foods become scarce. Lichens are slow-growers, often growing as little as two-tenths of an inch per year. Some lichens are over a thousand years old!

Over the ages, lichens have been used by people in many ways. The most famous use is the development of litmus paper, used to detect acidity. Lichens have been used in perfumes, potpourris, and dyes. They've also been used in cultures worldwide to treat various ailments. Today they are being studied as a potential new antibiotic, with one source stating that some lichen compounds have been found to be more effective than penicillin.

As you enter the world of lichens, you begin to discover a seemingly new dimension of life that was nearly invisible to you before you began your adventure. The more you find, the better your eyes become at recognizing new species. Unfortunately, there aren't many books to help you put a name to the lichens you find. Most people would find the lichen books that do exist to be too bulky, too expensive, or too technical to take to the field. Since lichens are so obscure, very few of them even have common names. But since nature's mysteries beg to be studied and understood, I think that some day Myakka will have a lichen list and that someone will publish a field guide to the lichens of Florida that any hiker, camper, or adventurer can take to the woods.

# Adventure 6

# Puzzles, Palms, and Pollinators

*"I once had a second-story window, when I lived on the bay in Sarasota, which was at the same level as the sabal palm spikes. In the winter, migrating cedar waxwings came in big flocks to eat the berries; other birds ate them too. It is sad how landscapers trim them all off."*
Jean Huffman

## Part 1: Puzzles and Palms

The challenge of this puzzle is to find the oldest trees in the forest. Before you select that tall, stately pine at the hammock's edge or the prodigious, sprawling live oak by the river, consider for a moment the little sabal palm. The sabal palm, or cabbage palm, is the most common palm in Florida. It grows farther north than any other native palm and is the only palm tree native to Myakka. It thrives in sun or shade, in times of flood or drought, and in Florida's infertile, sandy soils. It can withstand a raging fire though the entire tree may be engulfed by flames. If it is knocked over by a storm, it lives on, turning up and growing toward sunlight. No wonder it was designated Florida's State Tree by the legislature in 1953.

The cabbage palm is named for its best-known product: the heart of the bud. It is eaten raw or cooked like cabbage. It is quite time-consuming to prepare (especially if you had to cut down the tree with an ax), but it was once considered a staple in pioneers' diets. A book about Sarasota's first residents quoted a young girl who wrote of eating nothing but "swamp cabbage" and smoked mullet for breakfast, lunch, and dinner since her arrival in the state.

Early Floridians found many other uses for the tree as well. They reduced dried fruits to a coarse meal that was made into bread. The fresh pith was used by the Seminoles to make a pumpkinlike pie. They also obtained salt from the tree by a process similar to obtaining potash from wood. Palm-log huts used by medicine men were described by the Spanish, and many a pioneer weathered storms and eked out a living in shacks made from a frame of saplings covered with palm leaves.

The tree changes in appearance as it ages. Young seedlings look similar to palmettos. As the tree grows its bottom leaves drop off, leaving the hard, brown bases of the leaf stalks encircling the trees. These are often referred to as "boots." People say the term was derived from the way early Florida Crackers employed the broken-off appendages to remove their boots. Older cabbage palms usually lose all of their boots, leaving a relatively smooth trunk.

Wildlife are dependent on this versatile tree for food and shelter. Birds and other animals feed on the small berries that turn black and ripen in the winter. The boots and dead trees are composed of brown fibers that are used by animals for building nests and lining dens. Ferns take root in the humus that collects at the base of the boots, and rain collects in the pockets to provide water for wildlife. Be careful when brushing against the undersides of the fronds, as wasps also find them to be a good place to build their nests.

The challenge with this little tree is in determining its age. Like grasses or corn, the sabal palm grows upward from a single terminal bud and grows outward from the many bundles of tissues located in the center of the trunk. This is unlike most trees, which form annual growth rings, which can often be used to determine the age of the tree. So there is no way to estimate the exact age of a cabbage palm. When Florida was surveyed in the 1840s, large trees were marked to describe locations. Historians who retrace those surveys today find that the oaks and pines are often long gone, but the stalwart cabbage palms remain.

Since the growth rate of this palm is so variable, you can't assume that a short palm with all of its protruding boots is younger or older than its tall, smooth-trunked neighbor as each tree loses its boots at a different rate than another. But there is a way to estimate which trees are older. Palms always grow toward sunlight. If they encounter the canopy of an oak or another palm, they turn and grow around it. Lone palms in a prairie grow short, straight, and fat. There is no need to grow tall with no competition for sunlight.

In 1946, someone took a photograph of the river just behind the log pavilion. One stunted, mature sabal palm stood on the bank. Thirty years later, someone shot the same scene. The little palm looked as if it had not aged a day, but other trees had grown around it. A sapling oak had overtaken the palm and formed a canopy above it. Cabbage palms that were the size of palmetto bushes in the '46 photo ducked around the oak and overshot the little palm by fifteen feet. By the time I photographed the scene in the 1990s, several more new recruits were towering over the little palm. But each one had recorded the maximum height of its older neighbor by bending away from the older palm's canopy, snaking around its head, then reaching straight for open sky.

You can compare the relative ages in a group of trees that includes sabal palms by tracing the route the heads of the palms took on their journey through the canopy. Look for clues in the bends in the trunks of palms. What were they navigating around? Find the bootless, straight-trunked, shorter palms to determine those that may have grown in clearings without any competition.

## Part 2: Palms and Pollinators

My favorite time to observe cabbage palms is when they are in bloom. Fragrant, creamy-white blossoms cascade haphazardly from huge bloom stalks in late spring or summer. What I find fascinating about these flower clusters is the amount and variety of pollinators they attract. Bees, flies, wasps, beetles—a wild array of colorful, buzzing, flying creatures. I want to buy expensive photography equipment to stop each little green and blue and orange body in motion and study it carefully. I delight in pausing to count the number of different species I can pick out at one time at a single bloom stalk. And now that the canopy walkway and tower have been built, it is even easier to observe them up close.

If you have not yet discovered the world of pollinators, there is a wonderful book by Stephen L. Buchmann and Gary Paul Nabhan entitled *The Forgotten Pollinators* (Island Press, 1996). Once you read it, you will see our natural world and its insect life in a completely different light. In fact, I found it to be the most enlightening book I have read in years.

**Palm blossom**

# Adventure 7

## Shady Walks

Sometimes you want to take a walk in the shade. Shade is pretty easy to find along Park Drive since most of the park's paved roadway runs through hammock. But for those of you who enjoy a challenge and the diversity of exploring something new, I have compiled a list of shady walks off the beaten path. Many of them are areas that most park visitors would never discover on their own. I'll begin with the easiest routes to locate and move on to the more obscure locations (see the map on page 147). For all of these adventures, be sure to take a compass.

**Short River Walk:** There is a large pavilion by the river at the South Picnic area just inside the S.R. 72 park gate. The trail goes from the pavilion toward S.R. 72. You can take a short walk while the rest of your party picnics or fishes at the river. It is also a great place to do some birding. Be careful, there is quite a bit a poison ivy. Most of it grows as groundcover and can be easily avoided if you realize it is there.

**Nature Trail:** The Boylston Nature Trail (hammock trail) is located about a mile into the park. Go over the park bridge and around a couple of more bends in the road until you reach the nature trail sign. The circular trail is a leisurely forty-five-minute walk if you stop to read the trail signs. The signs tell about hammock inhabitants and the many ways they must adapt to survive the harsh environment of shade, flood, and drought. A spur trail off the loop takes you to the canopy walkway and tower.

**River Walk:** Drive over the park bridge and park on the far side in the parking lot. An interpretive sign describing some animals that live in the park marks the beginning of the trail. The trail was established over the years as fishermen and other park visitors walked along the riverbank. It floods in the summer but is a pleasant hike when the ground is dry. Return along the same route (unless you have a compass with you and don't mind maneuvering through or around head-high palmettos). You could think of this is as a multipurpose trail because you can take a hike, bird along the river, or cast your line and catch a fish at your whim.

**Alligator Point:** From the S.R. 72 park entrance, go about a quarter mile until you reach the second dirt road on the left. (Cabin Road is across the drive on the right.) Park on the road shoulder. The dirt road heads west for a few feet and then runs north and south at the west fence line. Take the right turn. There is a chain across the road but it is easy to walk around. The dike road runs along the west side of the river for a couple of miles to Alligator Point. You can identify the spot by the ninety-degree left turn in the road just where it intersects a bend in the river. The area has been called Alligator Point for as long as anyone can remember. True to its name, this spot usually has several alligators basking in the sun when the weather is cool enough or submerged with snouts protruding in warmer weather. A huge, old oak tree sprawls out over the river and each year gets closer to falling into the water.

If you walk farther, the road takes you to the power line, the location of the old railroad bridge. I find the bridge foundation interesting to explore. Continue past the power line and you will eventually reach Vanderipe Dike. The huge earthen structure was installed to reduce the amount of water in the slough and allow a large subdivision to be built along it many years ago. The hammock between the dike and the power line holds a few interesting features to discover. I have found rouge plant in berry (a plant rarely found in the park), silo foundations, an old artesian well, barred owls, and flocks of turkeys in the area. Return to your vehicle by the same route you came.

**Enchanted Forest:** The hammock across the weir is dark and mysterious. Because it was my son's favorite shady place to explore as a child, I often chose it as a destination when leading school groups. Its inaccessibility when the river flows over the weir and its eerie ambience inspired me to make up stories for children about it and name it the Enchanted Forest. To get there, go back to the swing sets behind the park concession and take the path that goes into the hammock. Walk over the concrete weir. (Don't try this when the surface is wet, however, since it can be very slippery.)

Walk through the hammock or along the forest edge. You can follow the lakeshore to a cove that is very popular with migrating waterfowl in the winter and early spring. If you follow the shore, eventually you will arrive at Vanderipe Dike. For an extended walk, you can circle to your left when you reach the dike and cut through the hammock to Alligator Point Road, thereby combining two different shady walks to make a very long one. If you end up on Park Drive at the parking place described in the Alligator Point walk, you will find yourself a good three miles from the park concession.

**Mossy Hammock Trail:** The closest primitive campground to the trailhead of the Myakka Trail is Mossy Hammock. It is a shady, two-and-a-half-mile hike from North Drive by way of the hiking trail. The campground is a great place for a picnic lunch. Then you can either return by the same route or take Mossy Hammock Road, High Road, and Fox's Low Road back to the trailhead. The roads are sunny, so on a hot day take the roads to the campground and return by way of the trail. The cutoff from Mossy Hammock Road to the trail will be difficult to find unless you have previously located it by taking the trail to where it passes within a few feet of the road.

**Sumeral Ponds:** Clarence Sumeral's grandfather lived at Bee Island. A trip to grandfather's house meant meandering around a large group of seasonal ponds before breaking out into open prairie to travel the last leg of the journey to the pines. In those days, the cluster of wetlands was known as Sumeral Ponds. I'm always delighted to discover someone who spent time in Myakka in the early part of the twentieth century, as I take every opportunity to piece together its history. So Clarence was a real treasure. Though I learned quite a bit from our discussion, I've always wished I had asked him more about his grandfather's place and those sojourns to the pinewoods before he passed away. Now I continue to pass on the legacy of the place name Sumeral Ponds by mentioning it to park visitors and each new ranger.

Al Cook, a ranger who retired in the early 1980s, told me that when he was a young ranger the ponds were open water most of the year and were one of his favorite fishing destinations. As I look out over the grassy wetlands in the spring, I try to imagine how much they have changed. A friend once told me that she found a water hickory growing on the far side of one of those ponds. I've never seen water hickory in the park, so each time I pass through the area I scan the distant marsh edge for wispy leaves and vow to return someday to explore the shady pond edges in hopes of locating that mystery tree. You can find Sumeral Ponds by walking out on Ranch House Road a little over two miles. The road passes through the intersection of the three marshes that make up Sumeral Ponds. Be sure to let me know if you find that tree.

**Lower Lake:** The shoreline of Myakka's smaller lake is surrounded by marsh and hammock, so as long as the water level is not high, it's a nice place to walk in the shade. The typical route to Deep Hole is on the west side of the river and is a sunny mile-and-a-half walk to the lakeshore. The route I like to take is more challenging. Go east on S.R. 72 from the park entrance to the second bridge, which crosses over the Myakka River. Cross the river bridge, take off your shoes, and wade across the ditch along the highway. You can tell it's dry enough when the water in the ditch along the highway is only knee-deep. Put on your shoes, veer to the right, and follow the hammock line south, skirting wet marshes and sloughs. When you reach the lakeshore, just follow the shoreline until you are ready to return. If at any time you feel lost, you can just head north until you reach S.R. 72. (Be sure to get a wilderness permit from the Ranger Station anytime you plan to explore the area south of S.R. 72, whether on foot or by boat. The area was designated a wilderness preserve when the land was acquired for the park in the 1930s.)

**Cypress Swamp:** Since the consensus among those who know the flora of the area is that cypress trees are not native to Sarasota County, when you find cypress trees here you can usually assume they were planted. But I know of a cypress head in Myakka that was not planted. It's in the Wilderness Preserve across from the entrance to Myakka Valley subdivision. A path that runs along the east side of a borrow pit pond (probably dug for fill when the highway was paved) takes you to a very nice cypress stand. These large trees are covered with butterfly orchids, which are beautiful in June when they are all in bloom. Of course you can expect to be wading knee-deep in swamp water that time of year, with mosquitoes buzzing around your head. But some years the rains begin later, delaying the arrival of the hatching mosquitoes.

When I began to work at Myakka in 1980, the district manager was Major Paul Walker. (Those were the days when the park service used military titles for anyone above ranger level.) Though he seemed ancient to me, he was probably born around 1910. When questioned about the origin of the cypress swamp across from Myakka Valley, he said that when he was a young boy there was only one big old cypress tree in a marsh at that location. Old maps show that an old wagon road passed along that marsh, so perhaps a wagon traveling through the area sometime back in the 1800s dropped a seed that was the beginning of the only cypress swamp in Sarasota County not actually planted by people.

**Isolated Hammocks:** The last two shady walks are the most challenging and are best attempted by those of you who know Myakka well, have explored its roads and trails, and hunger for fresh adventure. For this walk, begin by examining the habitat map in the Visitor Center or obtaining aerial photographs of the Myakka area. Since natural hammocks often form on the north side of large wetlands, the best way to explore remote, less-traveled hammocks is to locate them on the map, then navigate around or through a wetland during the dry season and find your own hammock to explore. Try this in the spring before it gets too hot: not only will you have to cross a sunny wetland, you may also have to hike quite a distance to reach your hammock. Searching out and locating these hidden hammocks is sure to bring out the "Lewis and Clark" in anyone adventurous enough to try. Don't forget to bring plenty of water.

**Hickory Hammock:** I saved my favorite for last. It's in the Wilderness Preserve on the east side of the river, south of S.R. 72 so you'll need a wilderness permit. The gate is about a mile east of the S.R. 72 park entrance. If you park there, do not block the entrance. Walk west along the north fence line until you reach a small cypress swamp (planted by CCC workers or early park rangers). Follow the road along the south side of the cypress head. After you pass the cypress, you will see very tall palmettos on your left bordering a hammock. Choose a point to cut into the woods where it looks like the shortest distance between the road and the trees and where the palmetto is less dense. I can usually find a place that is only about thirty feet of palmetto to plow through.

What I like about this hammock is its diversity. It doesn't flood and it supports more tree species than any hammock of its size in the park. You'll find pignut hickory, mulberry, live oak, laurel oak, marlberry, myrsine, sabal palm, holly, dogwood, cherry laurel, citrus, lime prickly ash, white stopper, viburnum, firebush, and wax myrtle. One of the Myakka old-timers told me that the ditches surrounding the hammock were dug by Sarasota County Mosquito Control workers in the 1950s. Each time I explore the area I think I may discover a new plant that I have not found there before. ❧

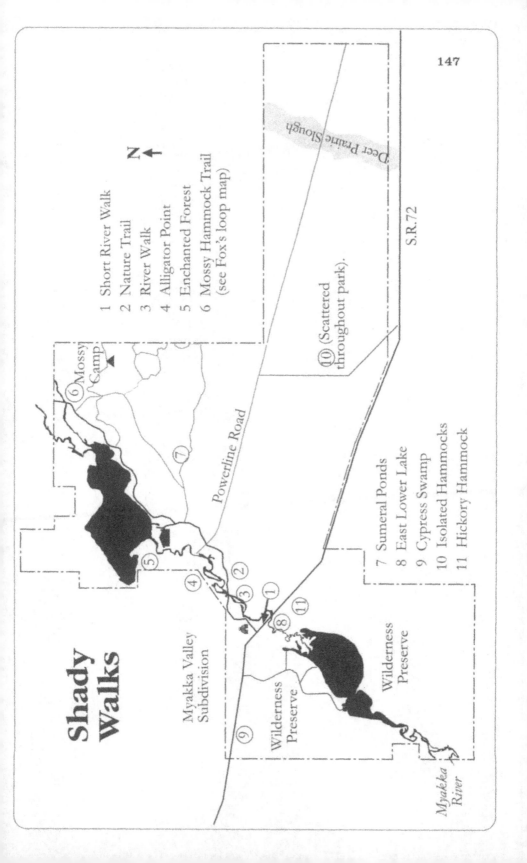

# Shady Walks

Myakka Valley Subdivision

Wilderness Preserve

Wilderness Preserve

*Myakka River*

Powerline Road

Mossy Camp

Deer Prairie Slough

S.R. 72

N

1 Short River Walk
2 Nature Trail
3 River Walk
4 Alligator Point
5 Enchanted Forest
6 Mossy Hammock Trail
  (see Fox's loop map)

7 Sumeral Ponds
8 East Lower Lake
9 Cypress Swamp
10 Isolated Hammocks
11 Hickory Hammock

⑩ (Scattered throughout park).

# 8

# Myakka by Starlight

Have you ever photographed a sunrise or the shimmering morning light through a dew-coated spider web? Have you called up an owl or shined gators on a misty lakeshore? Canoed a river or taken a bicycle ride by the light of the full moon? Myakka by night is entirely different from Myakka by day. Nocturnal animals stroll boldly to ponds and lakes, the sky is filled with a bounty of stars unseen in city light, and the night air comes alive with a cacophony of sounds.

Sensations seem more acute in the night air. It's as if all of your senses are honed to detect every clue around you. Perhaps it is the moisture in the air that intensifies sounds and smells. Your vision sharpens unimaginably as your eyes adjust to low light. Even your taste buds are enhanced. Just cook something over an open fire by starlight and compare the taste to anything you eat from your kitchen table.

Probably the most exciting facet of the Myakka night experience is the animal life. Even children know that most animals sleep by day and come out at night. So spending a night in the park is an exciting opportunity to look for those mysterious night creatures. But don't expect it to come too easily. The most thrilling discoveries require some serious sleuthing on your part mixed with a good bit of luck. If you are patient, observant, and open to adventure, you won't go home disappointed.

You'll increase your chances of finding the greatest diversity of animals if you take some time to learn about the habits of Myakka's nocturnal critters. For instance, bobcats favor established trails and are creatures of habit. So if you find bobcat scat on a dirt road or along a marsh edge during the day, you'll have a better chance of finding the animal if you return to the same location just after sunrise or sunset. Deer often graze in marshes, so bring a bright flashlight and shine it out over Big Flats Marsh after dark. Frogs are more active on warm, humid nights. Crayfish are on the move after a heavy rain. Otters are seen most often in the early morning hours and spend more time near the lakes when the water level is low. When the park begins to flood, they're on the move so you're more likely to see them on roads and trails and in ditches. You'll find the greatest concentration of alligators in the lakes and river in spring when the ponds and marshes begin to dry up.

Another way to enhance your animal detective skills is to learn to identify night sounds. Begin at the Visitor Center, where frog calls are just a push-button away. You can also purchase some excellent recordings of Florida bird and frog calls. (Lang Elliott has produced some great recordings of Florida birds, frogs, and other animals. Search the Internet for NatureSound Studio.) You can compare the list of sounds on your recording to the park's vertebrate list to make identification easier.

The Myakka Vertebrate List is helpful even if you don't have recordings. If you are walking on Park Drive along a hammock edge and you hear an owl call, you can look up the list of owls that live in hammocks in the park. The only choices are the screech owl and the barred owl. The barred owl, listed as abundant, is most common. It is also more vocal than the tiny screech owl. The animals on the list you are most likely to hear between sunset and sunrise are frogs, toads, alligators, raccoons, feral pigs, foxes, bobcats, coyotes, night herons,

**Black-crowned night heron**

whistling ducks, limpkins, owls, sandhill cranes, killdeer, whip-poor-wills, chuck-will's-widows, and mockingbirds. (See end of next section for a list of Myakka's nocturnal animals.)

## Spend the Night in Myakka

Most people who visit natural areas are more apprehensive about exploring them at night than during the day. But, surprisingly, it isn't wildlife that park visitors fear most during a night in the wilderness—it's people. The thought that someone would be more fearful of violence and crime in a remote area than in an urban area is surprising to those of us who live in Myakka. The only serious injuries that have occurred in the park that I know of were the result of automobile accidents.

As for people being injured by wildlife, the most serious injury I have heard of was of a man gored by a buck deer during rutting season in the 1950s. All three accounts of venomous snake bites since 1970 resulted from the victim's picking up or stepping on the snake.

One of the three incidents involved a diamondback rattlesnake that did not inject any poison into the boy who stepped on it.

Let me dispel the most infamous camp myths: snakes don't crawl into your bedroll at night, alligators don't roam the campground looking for a late-night snack, and feral hogs don't attack unless provoked. If you have any apprehensions about exploring Myakka at night, seek out a park ranger to discuss your concerns. You should, of course, use common sense whether you explore the wilds by day or night, but don't let your fears prevent you from experiencing Myakka by starlight.

To remain in the park after sunset, you can register to camp or purchase an annual entrance permit. Permit holders can obtain the gate combination and stay in the park as late as they desire. Permits may be purchased at any state park that offers camping.

If you plan to stay overnight in the park, you have several options. There are two family campgrounds, a group camp (that accommodates clusters of tents), and six primitive campgrounds located along the thirty-nine-mile hiking trail. The closest backpack sites are about a two-and-a-half-mile hike from the trailhead. There are also five log cabins with kitchens, fireplaces, and air conditioning. (See Myakka A–Z Appendix for information about camping and cabins.)

Another way to spend time at Myakka in the evening hours is to become a park volunteer. Volunteers are sometimes needed to work as camp hosts, to conduct frog chorus surveys, or to participate in other projects. Contact a park ranger or stop by the Ranger Station for more information.

Before you begin the night adventures on the following pages, you'll want to pack the proper accoutrements. A bright flashlight with extra batteries is the first thing on the list. You're less likely to disturb the wildlife you encounter if you either place a transparent red cover over the light or use a red light bulb. Many animals are unable to see red light.

Though you can learn to navigate using the night sky, be sure to bring a compass. It's easy to become disoriented in a hammock at night. The moon rises in the east and sets in the west just as the sun does and the constellations are as constant as they've always been, but you never know when sudden cloud cover will obscure the stars and moon. Moonrise and moonset tables are helpful. Most daily newspapers print this information on the weather or sports page. You can also check an almanac or search the Internet.

Whether you are exploring the woods by day or night, you can never have too many field guides (as long as you don't carry them with you on the trail). The most helpful guides for night adventures are the ones on frogs, mammals, and animal tracks.

Glow-in-the-dark spiders and luminescent mushrooms, cackles and roars, whistles and screeches—all add to the mystery of the eerie night world and beckon you to a whole new set of adventures you can never experience by the light of day.

## Myakka's Nocturnal Animals

*Amphibians*
greater siren
peninsula newt
two-toed amphiuma
Eastern spadefoot toad
Southern toad
oak toad
greenhouse frog (non-native)
pinewoods treefrog
barking treefrog
squirrel treefrog
green treefrog
Cuban treefrog (non-native)
little grass frog
Southern chorus frog (also calls by day)
Florida cricket frog (also calls by day)
bullfrog
pig frog
Southern leopard frog

Florida gopher frog
Eastern narrow-mouth frog

*Reptiles*
American alligator
Indo-Pacific gecko (non-native)
striped crayfish snake
Florida water snake (also called banded water snake)
Eastern mud snake
red rat snake (corn snake)
yellow rat snake (nocturnal only in summer)
scarlet kingsnake
Florida scarlet snake
Florida cottonmouth
dusky pigmy rattlesnake
Eastern diamondback rattlesnake

*Birds*
- black-crowned night heron
- yellow-crowned night heron
- limpkin
- barn owl
- Eastern screech owl
- great horned owl
- barred owl
- chuck-will's-widow (summer resident)
- whip-poor-will (winter resident)
- common nighthawk

*Mammals*
- Virginia opossum
- Southeastern shrew
- short-tailed shrew
- least shrew
- Eastern mole
- evening bat
- Brazilian free-tailed bat
- nine-banded armadillo (non-native)
- Southern flying squirrel
- red fox (non-native)
- gray fox
- coyote (non-native)
- raccoon
- long-tailed weasel
- Eastern spotted skunk
- striped skunk
- bobcat
- Florida panther
- wild pig (non-native)

# Adventure 1

## Build a Fire

A camping excursion is somehow incomplete without a nice, cheery campfire to set the mood. But sometimes even park rangers fail to produce that perfect fire. I've heard of some who have used a blowtorch or a drip torch (designed for prescribed fire ignition) rather than face the humiliation of not having blazing flames ready for a campfire program.

Begin by bringing your own firewood or purchasing wood from the concession. (Park policy prevents collection of firewood in state parks.) Wad up a large piece of paper and cover it with dry, dead palm fronds. If you don't have any paper, you can just use the palm fronds. Stack finger-size twigs in the shape of a teepee around the palm fronds. (You can use the palm fronds alone, but paper improves your chances of success.) Build a larger teepee around the twigs with thumb-size, dry branches. Light the middle of your fire ring. As it blazes, gradually continue to add larger pieces of dry wood, enlarging the exterior of your teepee. It is always a challenge to try to get each additional piece of wood to stand upright rather than collapse the teepee. By the time you put the larger pieces of wood on the fire, the flames will be blazing brightly and it doesn't really matter if the teepee falls in.

## Of Stars and Fireballs
**This adventure was written by R. W. Dampman.**

Grab a flashlight and take a stroll where the sky is big and wide. The end of the lake parking lot is a good sky-watch location. So is the bird-walk. And if you're feeling courageous, the top of the canopy walkway tower adds a hint of thrill to this adventure. When you reach your chosen night-sky observation point, turn off the flashlight, wait a few minutes for your eyes to adjust to the darkness, take a breath, and look skyward. What do you see? Stars? Maybe a nice crescent moon? Not too much happening? Think again!

If you know where and how to look, you can see meteors, fireballs, comets, gas clouds, entire star nurseries, other worlds that turn science fiction into science fact, and more moons than you can shake a stick at. Sure, there's the occasional airplane, with its blinking red and green lights, but did you know you can also spot orbiting spacecraft and satellites? Not to mention all the stories and legends that come from the simple positions of the stars themselves! Not only is most of this happening on any given night, but much of it can be experienced with just the naked eye and a good star chart.

Satellites and spacecraft can be seen right after dark. The sun has already set for us, but to these orbiting objects high in the sky, the sun is very visible. So as the sun's light reflects off them we can easily see their reflection. They appear to be fast-moving airplanes, but with no sound or blinking lights.

As for constellations, one of the first to look for in the summer sky, after the sun is good and gone, is the Big Dipper. From Myakka, this fairly large constellation appears in the northern sky, about halfway up from the horizon. One of the more interesting things about this star group is the second star up on the handle. If you look carefully, you will see another very faint star right next to it. This is what's known as an optical binary star because though it appears as if the two stars orbit one another, the smaller star is really much farther out in space than the first. The real secret, though, is that the larger star is a true binary star itself. It has another star—too small to see with the naked eye—orbiting it! Try to find it with a telescope sometime.

The Little Dipper is pretty small in comparison to the Big Dipper. It's also closer to the horizon and can be hard to see as far south as Myakka River. A lot of people look for that ever-so-bright North Star. The North Star is actually pretty low in the sky this far south, and you may be surprised to discover that it is actually not all that bright.

During the winter months, one of the more impressive constellations is Orion the Hunter. A little smaller than the Big Dipper, it strolls across the night sky nearly overhead (just a little to the south). A good star chart will point out Orion's sword or belt. A strong pair of binoculars or small telescope will reveal that the middle star of his sword is not a star at all but actually a gaseous nebula. (A nebula is a region or cloud of interstellar dust and gas appearing as a hazy bright or dark patch.) Close by Orion is a fairly bright star that is the "eye" of Orion's hunting dog, Sirius.

Look a little farther to the west. You will see what looks like a Little Dipper but is actually a star group called the Pleiades. How many stars can you find. Six? Eight? Look again with your binoculars.

You should see dozens. Look with a telescope and you'll see hundreds! That's because the Pleiades is actually a cluster where stars are forming—right before your very eyes!

A good star book or atlas will provide the locations of the planets in our solar system. They travel through the sky at different speeds than the stars, so their position is always changing. Using your binoculars, it's possible to see a few of the moons around Jupiter and even the rings around Saturn. Look for Mars and Venus too.

A little time spent staring up into the night sky often provides glimpses of meteors and meteorites. A meteor is usually about the size of a softball while a meteorite can be as small as a pea. They move very fast through space and occasionally are pulled into the Earth's atmosphere, where the friction of the air causes them to burn up, giving us the little blips of light we call shooting stars. Every once in a while, a much larger piece comes down and burns its way across the entire sky. This is a fireball and is often quite spectacular.

Well, that should get you started. There is so much more. There's Cassiopeia, Hercules, Draco (the dragon), Berenice's hair—and when you start looking into the myths and stories attached to all these mysterious names, you'll discover yet another dimension of the night sky. So the next time you find yourself outside at night, take a moment, look up, and see who's out and about.

# Adventure 3

## The Frog Caper

**Green treefrog**

I find frogs to be captivating creatures. I love their beady little black eyes and marshmallow-soft bellies. I've always liked to watch treefrogs navigate across my windows at night with suction-cup toes. I used to turn on the outside lights to attract more bugs for them to devour. Sure, it was a nuisance to rescue them from behind the couch, where they'd gone to escape my cat, or to carefully corral an interloper who had claimed my shower. I didn't even mind when I had to put a pillow over my head at night to get some sleep as thousands upon thousands of them argued outside my window: "You did it. No, you did it. No, you did it!"

Sadly, the multitudes of frogs have disappeared from near my home, just as they have from many places all over the world. I don't know if it's because diligent mosquito exterminators have destroyed their prey or if the loss can be blamed on the many new residents of this once-remote portion of the county, armed with their arsenals of chemicals. Perhaps the little treefrogs have been consumed or out-competed by imported interlopers like the Cuban treefrog or the Indo-Pacific gecko. Maybe they have succumbed to the bombardment of UVB rays in our ozone-depleted atmosphere. For whatever reason, the great numbers of frogs are gone from my neighborhood, and I miss them.

At Myakka frogs still reign! There's no better place to become inti-mately acquainted with Florida's anuran species. Choose a warm, sum-mer evening just after a hard rain. I prefer to hunt along North Drive on weeknights because there are so few cars in summer and fall. You can imagine you're one of the only people in the park for long stretches of time. I turn on my bright headlights and drive slowly down the road, watching for little pebblelike or rocklike bumps on the pavement.

Each time I see something out of place on the smooth pavement, I jump out of the truck and shine my flashlight in the direction of the creature. Then I quickly close in for the catch. Actually, I rarely keep the little fellows. All I want to do is to identify them and then shoo them off the road. Sometimes I catch them and put them in a small plastic aquarium to photograph the next day. I try to find and identi-fy as many different kinds of frogs as I can in one evening.

A good field guide on frogs and toads makes this activity more fun. My favorite is *Handbook of Reptiles and Amphibians of Florida*, Part Three: *The Amphibians* by Ray E. Ashton Jr. and Patricia Sawyer Ashton (Windward Publishing, 1988). Not only does it provide pho-tographs of frogs and tadpoles, it also has range maps to tell you which frogs are likely to be found in the area in which you are frogging. Here are a few hints on identifying some of Myakka's frogs.

Though there is no scientific distinction between toads and frogs, creatures that hop (vertical and horizontal movement relatively equal) are usually named toads, and those that leap (with more forward than vertical movement) are called frogs. But sometimes even the experts disagree on nomenclature. The little narrow-mouth toad is identified in some books as a narrow-mouth frog. When you find a little fellow that hops like a toad, bleats like a goat, and looks like a frog with a pointed nose, it's a narrow-mouth frog (toad). Otherwise, since spadefoot toads are rarely encountered on the road, any other toad on Park Drive will probably be the little oak toad or common Southern toad. If it's bigger than a man's thumb, it's a Southern toad. If it's smaller, it's either a young Southern toad or a full-grown oak toad. If the critter is calling and sounds like a chick peeping loudly, it's an oak toad. If the call is more like an old-fashioned telephone ringing, it's a Southern toad.

Squirrel treefrogs and green treefrogs look very much alike: both are often green and about two inches long (though green treefrogs can grow over two inches long). But the green treefrog has a white, sharply defined stripe that runs under each eye and down each side of its body. The squirrel treefrog may have a faint stripe, but it does not extend along the length of its body. Both frogs can change colors from green to brown or gray-green.

Large frogs leaping across the drive are usually Southern leopard frogs, though I have discovered a few pig frogs on the road too. And although I have heard isolated calls from bullfrogs now and then, I have never found a bullfrog on the road.

As you travel along the road, you'll hear choruses of different frogs just waiting to be recognized. Spend some time beforehand in the Visitor Center, pushing the buttons on the frog display and listening to the calls to get acquainted with the different sounds. There are also recordings of frog calls and night sounds on tapes and CDs that can be a big help. (Try *The Calls of Frogs and Toads* by Lang Elliott, NatureSound Studio, 2000.) The more you train your ear, the better you'll be able to pick out the sounds of each type of frog in a large chorus.

Once you get to know Myakka's troubadours, you are likely to become a frog fan. What's a frog fan? A frog fan is someone who runs outside on a rainy night to find out which group is onstage for the evening, or sleeps with the windows open in hopes of being lulled to sleep by the *hum-drum* of a bullfrog or the maraca-like rhythm of the pinewoods treefrog. A frog fan anticipates that rare deluge of rain that awakens the spadefoot toad. Only a serious frog fan stalks through the piney woods on a crisp winter night listening for the breeding chorus of the Florida gopher frog, or knows the thrill of discovering a group of barking treefrogs baying at the moon.

**Leopard frog**

## Adventure 4

# Paddle and Pedal by the Light of the Moon

Here's an adventure for moderately experienced park visitors. To attempt this trip, you should be very familiar with Park Drive and have canoed the river between the boat basin and the south picnic pavilion at least twice, preferably in the same season that your night adventure will occur. You should also be relatively comfortable around alligators. The animals don't pose a threat, but if you become startled and overreact at the splash of one close to your canoe, you could capsize your boat.

The activity involves a two-hour (or more) canoe trip from Upper Myakka Lake, down river to the south picnic pavilion, and a bicycle ride back to the boat basin parking lot. Planning is very important, as timing will most influence your level of success. Success is measured only by how much pleasure you get from the venture.

You will need a canoe (with paddles and vest-type life jackets) and a bicycle for each person in your party. Bicycles can be rented overnight from the park concession. You also need to get a recreational use permit or register to camp. You don't have to spend the night in the campground. You can pay the camp fee just to stay in the park after hours.

The best time of the year for this activity is probably a matter of personal preference. Some prefer the summer when the water is high. The current will make the trip faster, unless you are delayed by taking a wrong turn. As the river meanders through Big Flats Marsh just south of the weir, it can get tricky with so many dead-end channels. The last time I took this night trip, the water level was moderately high and I confidently followed the widest channel until I came up against a wall of West Indian marshgrass. At first I thought a mat of floating grass had blocked the main river channel and I would have to cancel my trip. But when I backtracked, I discovered a narrow path about six feet wide that went all the way through. The widest trail is not always the main channel.

Of course, you'll have to contend with mosquitoes during summer trips. I find them most intense in September, especially just after sunset. Most people bring lots of mosquito spray. I prefer long pants, socks covering my ankles, a long-sleeve silk shirt, and a hat with a mosquito net. If there's a breeze, I don't need to use the net.

If you choose to do the trip other times of the year, the current is so slow that it is the wind that most influences your rate of travel. This portion of the river is not often blocked by water hyacinths, but there is always the possibility. A day trip will provide valuable insight into the river conditions. In October and November, the water level is still relatively high from summer rains, and there is a noticeable decrease in mosquitoes.

A full moon will give you plenty of light by which to navigate the river. Check an almanac, a newspaper, a calendar, or the Internet to determine the date of the full moon. The full moon rises at about the same time the sun sets. It takes five to seven hours (depending on the time of year) for the moon to be directly overhead. So if you plan a summer trip, realize that the moon doesn't rise until after 8:00 P.M. That will put it overhead in the early morning hours. If you are not a night owl but want to experience a bright, moonlit sky, choose a night a couple of days before the full moon. Be sure to check the weather report too. It won't matter how bright the moon is if the sky is covered by clouds.

It is the challenge of navigating Big Flats Marsh that makes the trip time difficult to estimate. The more times you have to retrace your path to locate the main channel, the longer it will take to complete the trip. It is more difficult to navigate the marsh paddling upstream than downstream, so if you plan to return to your origin by canoe instead of bicycle, be sure to make note of the false streams coming into the river so you can find your way back more easily.

Whether or not to use a flashlight on your trip may be a difficult choice. The longer your eyes adjust to the lack of artificial light, the better your night vision. But the urge to identify the source of the splash close to your canoe, the birds muttering in their sleep from riverside roosts, or the frog calling from the bank may be more than you can resist. Besides, you can't shine for gators without a flashlight!

Estimates of the park's alligator populations are done routinely, with night forays down the river by Florida Fish and Wildlife Conservation Commission biologists. Of course, all that is gained is an estimate of the number of alligators in the river and lakes. There are thousands of wetlands where alligators dwell throughout the fifty-eight square miles of state park–managed land. To count the alligators along your route like the census takers do, just shine a bright flashlight along the water's surface. As you look down the beam of light, you will see pairs of glowing, red eyes wherever the reptiles are resting. Don't expect your companion to see the red eyes, though. You must be looking directly down the light beam to see them.

When all your planning is done and the big night of your adventure arrives, here's how to put it all together. Deliver the required number of bicycles to the south pavilion by the river. Take your canoe up to the boat basin and launch it from the area beside the canoe rack or at the boat ramp. Lock your vehicle and leave it in the boat basin parking lot.

Canoe from the lake, over the weir (or portage around), down the river, under the Myakka River Bridge, and on until you get to the south picnic area pavilion. Pull the canoe up into the picnic area and pick up your bicycles. Though I enjoy the canoe trip, I like the bicycle ride back even better. All that is left to do when you reach your vehicle is to return to the picnic area to pick up your canoe.

I have one last hint for anyone who tires of paddling before reaching the end of the route. You can leave the canoe at the park bridge and walk to the south pavilion. This also adds variety to the trip by including a short hike with the paddle-and-pedal adventure.

Here are some other suggestions for night adventures:

- Bike to Mossy Hammock and camp at the primitive campground
- Attend a park campfire program
- Purchase an owl call and call up a barred owl
- Fish from a park bridge
- Learn to orient yourself by the moon and stars
- Hike the nature trail
- Go stargazing
- Bicycle or skate North Drive
- Watch a sunrise from the canopy walkway tower or birdwalk
- Go gator shining with a flashlight
- Use a star wheel (A star wheel is a cardboard circle of star fields with a clear overlay that you turn to line up dates and times to find out where to look for specific stars and constellations.)
- Tell ghost stories around a big campfire (The Campfire Circle behind the log restroom is a great location for it.)

# Adventure
# 5

## The Sound of Spadefoot Toads

This adventure was written by Jean Huffman, park biologist
at Myakka River State Park from 1987 until 1995.

**Spadefoot toad**

When I lived in Myakka River State Park, I often listened to the many
kinds of frog calls. The Hill Residence area where I lived was, as the
name implies, relatively high and dry, though there were ponds nearby
and I could often hear choruses of frogs in the distance. But one night
I was surprised when my little trailer on the hill was at the center of the
loudest chorus of frogs I had ever heard. The deafening chorus outside
my door was not the sound of any frog or toad I recognized. I went outside and examined a few of the hundreds of animals making this incred-
ible sound. They were small toads (two to three inches long) with no
warts and distinctive vertical pupils. The spadefoot toads had emerged!

Later, I had to put the pillow over my head to try to sleep. The blaring sound outside continued throughout the night. That day, heavy rains had flooded the dirt road and surrounding areas. The rains had been heavy enough to inspire the spadefoot toads (who live most of their lives underground) to surface and join a mating frenzy. These toads emerge only after a nocturnal summer deluge forms pools of water in upland areas that are normally quite dry. They call, mate, and lay eggs, which need only two days to hatch. The tadpoles change into land-dwelling toads in as little as ten days.

It is a real treat to see spadefoot toads, since they are much more difficult to find than the other types of frogs and toads that live at Myakka. Most of their time is spent in subterranean burrows. The spadelike projections on their hind feet allow them to dig into the soil quite easily. During extended drought periods, spadefoot toads can even become dormant underground. They curl up and excrete a fluid that hardens the soil around them, making a small chamber that retains moisture. When heavy rains soak the soil, the toads move out of their chambers and resume their normal activities.

The mass emergence of the breeding spadefoot toads is a real event and a challenging Myakka adventure. It usually occurs only once or twice a year. It's a challenge because there is no way to know in advance when the next spadefoot gathering will take place. When the conditions seem right—that is, when the barometer drops and heavy rains pass through the area—come out to the park and listen in upland areas. A few suggested places to listen are off of S.R. 72 between the west park entrance sign and the park gate; the Bee Island Campground (three miles down Ranch House Road); and the south picnic area just inside the south park entrance. You can purchase a recreational use permit and stay as late as you want. If you're lucky enough to hear the honking roar of a full chorus of spadefoot toads, it's something you'll long remember.

One word of caution: If you handle a spadefoot toad, you should wash your hands well afterwards. Many people are sensitive to the toads' skin secretions, and some have allergic reactions to them. ❧

## 9

# The Myakka Island

A satellite image of Florida reveals the transformation of land cover that has occurred in just a few decades in this state. Had such technology been available in the 1950s, we would have seen a sea of wilderness with islands of agriculture and development plopped in strategic locations, especially along the coast. Now the image depicts the results of Florida's unprecedented, rampant growth—islands of wilderness, large and small, scattered across a peninsula of urban and suburban development, linked by agricultural lands.

The Myakka Island is one of those green spots. The first time I heard the term "Myakka Island" was in the early 1990s, when a residential development containing over six thousand homes was planned along the park's southern border. Now the Myakka Island is loosely defined as the remaining native habitat in the Myakka watershed. The Southwest Florida Water Management District (SWFWMD) staff estimated that about sixty percent of the watershed's 600 square miles

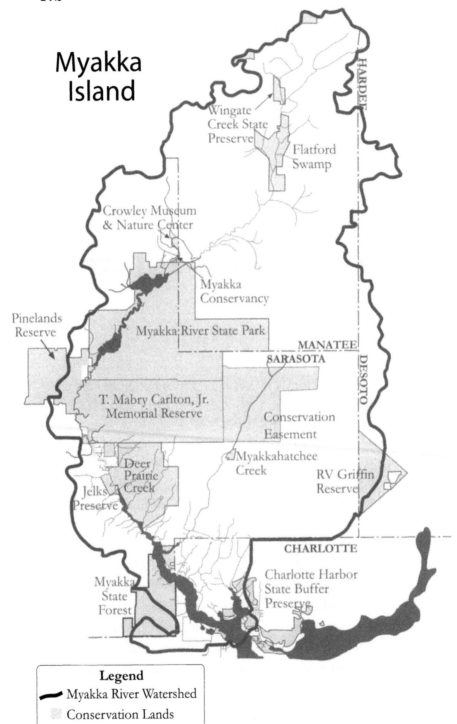

# Myakka
Island

Wingate
Creek State
Preserve

Flatford
Swamp

HARDEE

Crowley Museum
& Nature Center

Myakka
Conservancy

Pinelands
Reserve

Myakka River State Park

MANATEE

SARASOTA

DESOTO

T. Mabry Carlton, Jr.
Memorial Reserve

Conservation
Easement

Deer
Prairie
Creek

Myakkahatchee
Creek

RV Griffin
Reserve

Jelks
Preserve

CHARLOTTE

Myakka
State
Forest

Charlotte Harbor
State Buffer
Preserve

## Legend
➤ Myakka River Watershed
⬚ Conservation Lands

was still relatively natural in 2000. That is remarkable considering the amount of growth the state has experienced in the last twenty years.

It means that there is a chance for saving enough land to preserve a somewhat naturally functioning ecosystem—a chance that has been lost for many other parts of our state. Large contiguous chunks of land such as the Myakka Island are increasingly rare and vulnerable to Florida's rapid growth. The Myakka Island is one of the last remaining large wilderness areas in southwest Florida acquired and managed in perpetuity as a natural ecosystem. Its pieces are still being collected and put together in hopes of saving enough land.

But how much land is enough? How many acres does it take to support a Florida panther? How many individual animals are needed to sustain a population of bears or bobcats? How large an area will ensure the long-range survival of the Myakka ecosystem? Those questions are becoming more important each day as what was once miles and miles of endless wilderness is transformed into housing developments, schools, churches, and intensive agricultural operations. As a sea of development surrounds the native land that remains, the Myakka Island becomes susceptible to some of the same perils as an island in the middle of an ocean.

Islands are unique and complex ecosystems that are extremely vulnerable to outside influences. Entire populations of plants and animals can be wiped out by what appear to be minor disturbances. If a population of plants or animals on the island is suddenly reduced by a natural occurrence (such as a hurricane or disease) to a level too low to maintain a viable population, there are no other populations to draw from. (A viable population is ample unrelated individuals necessary to perpetuate their kind.) The threat of extinction is further intensified when introduced species (such as humans with their pets and exotic diseases) arrive on the island. Native species that evolved without contact with these new organisms are often unable to compete or defend themselves.

Just as an island must provide all that is needed for the survival of its inhabitants, an island of wilderness surrounded by developed land must contain sufficient quality habitat to support all of its plants and animals. The challenge isn't just to have enough land to sustain each individual: there must also be enough area to maintain viable populations of all the species that depend on each other for survival.

A single Florida panther requires forty-five to two hundred square miles (depending on quality of habitat) for its territory. Panthers are solitary animals. They will not tolerate another individual in their territory except during mating season. Even a female will not allow her offspring to remain in her territory once they have matured. The entire Myakka watershed contains only about 600 square miles, or 384,000 acres. Most people are shocked to discover that the combined acreage of all the pieces of land that form the Myakka Island is not large enough to support Florida panthers.

Florida black bears require large, undeveloped woodland tracts with a variety of different kinds of vegetation. The home range of an adult bear varies from an average of eleven square miles for females to fifty-four square miles for adult males. Scientists estimate that an area of 750 to 1,500 square miles is necessary to support a viable population of Florida black bears.

Even smaller carnivores need substantial territory in order to survive. The home range of a male bobcat averages 7.5 square miles. About 4.5 square miles are required for a female. Bobcats require a mix of habitats, such as hardwood swamps, pine flatwoods, and marshes, so the kind of space is as important as the amount of space. And like panthers, bobcats are not likely to share their space. Except when adults come together to mate or when a female is raising kittens, bobcats remain alone throughout their lives. Juveniles evicted from their mothers' home range may remain at the edge of that range for a month or two but must eventually strike out to claim their own territory. Juvenile bobcats can travel as far as 113 miles over several months before finding a vacant home range in which to settle.

The quality of habitat is also an important consideration. It is estimated that a one-year-old female bobcat and her three kittens will consume at least thirty-eight hundred cotton rats, thirty-two hundred cotton mice, and seven hundred cottontail rabbits by the end of the mother's second year. All of this prey must be within the home range that she shared with an adult male during mating season and with all the other predators (e.g., birds, snakes, foxes, coyotes) using her range. Consider the consequences of a delay in burning for a year or two. Since most of Myakka's fire-dependent habitats require fire every two to three years to stay healthy, each additional year that burning is postponed results in a drop in the number of prey the land can support. When burning authorizations are denied for nearly the entire burn season for three sequential years (such as occurred in 1999, 2000, and 2001), the effects reverberate through the entire ecosystem.

Some animals have very specific needs in terms of habitat. Red-cockaded woodpeckers require mature pine forests with an open understory maintained by fire. Grasshopper sparrows can reproduce only in grassy dry prairie that has been burned within the past two years. Though these two endangered species were lost during the decades Myakka was deprived of fire, we hope one day they will be reintroduced to Myakka. In the meantime, we must pay attention to the special needs of each of Myakka's inhabitants, whether it's frequent fire for grass-grazing tortoises, growing-season burns for scrub jays, or naturally fluctuating water levels for wading birds.

Wading birds feed in the river and lakes during the winter and spring but move to the isolated wetlands when water levels drop. They also build their rookeries in prairie and flatwoods ponds. Some frogs reproduce only in ponds that dry up in the winter. And a good-size piece of scrub habitat is necessary to support enough families of scrub jays to maintain a viable population. So you can see that it is not just the number of acres that is important but what those acres contain.

A wilderness island must also contend with development along its borders. Homes bring typical threats such as herbicide and pesticide use, invasive plants, and ditching and other alterations in land elevations that affect water flow patterns. But many other problems also arise as former city-dwellers become natural areas' neighbors. Traditionally, Florida's large natural lands were bordered by low-intensity agricultural land such as cattle ranches. But as housing developments pop up along fence lines, land managers must contend with a whole new set of challenges.

For instance, the impact of dogs and cats on native wildlife would be unbelievable to most people. One housecat in the vicinity of scrub can destroy an entire community of scrub jays, and studies of ground-nesting birds show devastating losses in areas that border urban settings. Then there are the critters you might call the shy animals, species that are more sensitive to human presence than others. Animals like eagles, white- and swallow-tailed kites, wood ducks, panthers, bears, and weasels reproduce successfully only in wilderness situations. Animals that adapt and even benefit from human habitation, such as rats, starlings, armadillos, opossums, and raccoons, increase as borders develop. This spells doom not only for the shy animals with which they compete, but also for ground-nesting birds, reptiles, and amphibians, whose nests are plundered by these interlopers.

As the number of homes built along wildland borders increases, so does the risk of disease. Feline panleukopenia, which can be from domestic cats, is thought to be the cause of the near decimation of a population of bobcats in south central Florida.

Smoke management during ecological burns also becomes a greater problem when homes border natural areas. Homeowners don't want smoke blowing their way. But if all sides of a park are occupied by homes, burn managers can no longer plan fires to send the smoke over unpopulated areas. The more complaints the Division of Forestry receives about smoke, the greater the pressure to require that burn zones be divided into smaller areas. Smaller burn zones require construction of new roads, which alter predator/prey relationships, increase exotic plant invasion, take more hours to maintain, and increase the number of burn days it takes to burn fire-dependent acreage.

The harder it becomes for land managers to burn, the further behind they get in burn goals. The longer land goes unburned, the more difficult it is to suppress a fire ignited by lightning or a prescribed fire that has blown off-course. This can be hazardous for homes built close to natural areas, especially if they are built in long-unburned, fire-dependent habitat. Head-high palmettos growing within a few feet of a residence are a disaster when the yard catches fire.

When Myakka River State Park was first acquired, no one imagined that its forty-one square miles would ever be considered not enough. Its wilderness seemed immense. But as Sarasota, Bradenton, North Port, and Arcadia grow closer together each year, we realize that the wilderness is no longer endless. In the 1980s, Sarasota County residents were presented with a bond issue to obtain the sixteen thousand acres south of the park. The area was touted as a future water source and as a haven for wildlife. A large color portrait of a Florida panther was brandished across a special edition of the *Sarasota Herald-Tribune* beseeching voters' approval. Fortunately, the bond was approved and the land was purchased. It is now known as the T. Mabry Carlton Jr. Memorial Reserve.

When land east of the park was threatened by development in 1992, thousands of Floridians wrote letters petitioning for its protection. The campaign was a success. Sarasota County partnered with SWFWMD to purchase the sixteen thousand acres. Nearly 8,000 acres were added to the Carlton Reserve, and the remaining 8,249 acres (called the Myakka Prairie) were turned over to the state park for management. If this sounds like a large chunk of the Myakka Island has been protected, consider that the total acreage of these three preserves is about sixty-two thousand acres. That's only about ninety-six square miles, perhaps enough land to support one Florida panther.

The Nature Conservancy popularized conservation easements as a method of preserving native ecosystems in the 1990s. Private landowners of large, healthy, natural areas sign an agreement to continue to manage their land in the same manner as they have in the past, thus preserving the integrity of the land. They are usually paid a substantial fee, but the cost is considerably less than the price of acquisition and the cost of future land-management activities. SWFWMD entered into a conservation easement with owners of the Carlton Ranch (east of Myakka River State Park and Myakka Prairie), thus ensuring that 4,997 acres of the ranch would always remain a part of the Myakka Island. Since that time, several other landowners have signed Conservation Easement agreements putting their land under the same blanket of protection.

By 2008, there were 251,000 acres (392 square miles) in public ownership, protected by conservation organizations or by conservation easement agreements. Sarasota County, SWFWMD, The Nature Conservancy, and Myakka River State Park have acquired land along the river corridor, placing long stretches, sometimes on both sides of the river, in public ownership. Voters in Sarasota County approved a continuation of the penny tax to extend the environmental lands program.

Only time will tell whether enough missing puzzle pieces will eventually be acquired to link the protected lands in the Myakka ecosystem or whether some parcels will eventually become small, isolated islands themselves. And even if the environmental lands purchase plans are a total success, large predators like the panther and black bear will still require more area than the size of any one island. That is why a system of corridors to connect wilderness islands throughout the state will be necessary if we want to give all of our wild things a chance for survival.

The Myakka Island is a mixture of private properties, large and small, and public lands purchased for different purposes and managed for varied goals. It contains an assortment of habitats, from mucky swamps and verdant marshes to rare and imperiled prairies and scrub. Its inhabitants are farmers, ranchers, conservationists, endangered scrub jays, common crows, slithering snakes, and insects and other pollinators that don't stand a chance in an urban environment. The Myakka Island is a haven for hikers, bikers, fishermen, canoeists, researchers, students, ecologists, and those of us who appreciate the simple wildness of wilderness. It is Myakka's size, complexity, and potential for preserving a functioning natural system that make it so valuable to our state. That is why all the managers of its fragmented pieces must work together to prevent the loss of its working components if we are to have any chance of ensuring the long-term survival of the Myakka ecosystem.

# Adventure 1

## The Myakka-Carlton Trail

In 2001, Sarasota County made the construction of several recreational trails throughout the county a priority. One of the first to be developed was a trail to connect Myakka River State Park, the Myakka Prairie, and the Carlton Reserve. The trail enables hikers, bicyclists, and horseback riders to travel among the three areas—well, at least during the drier times of the year. Trails through these public lands are usually too wet to travel during the summer rainy season.

The trail begins at the north gate of Myakka River State Park. The park's north entrance is located south and east of the east end of S.R. 780, about a mile past the Myakka River Bridge. The north gate is open for cars only weekends and state holidays, but there is a walk-through for hikers and bicyclists. You can park your car outside the gate, or, if you purchase an annual entrance permit, you can call the Ranger Station and obtain the gate combination. Only the portion of the trail south of the power line is open to horseback riders.

Trail signs will take you down the paved North Drive, onto Fox's High Road (one of the dirt access roads), down All Weather Road, east along S.R. 72, across the highway, through the Myakka Prairie portion of the park, and through the Carlton Reserve. The trail is twenty-two miles long but you can alter your route or add additional trails using the Myakka Wild & Scenic Trails Map. Trails on the map are color coded to identify use restrictions (for horses, bicycles, and hikers). You can pick up a map in the Ranger Station. A donation is requested, but not required, to fund subsequent printings of the map.

# Myakka-Carlton Trail
## Sarasota County Master Trail

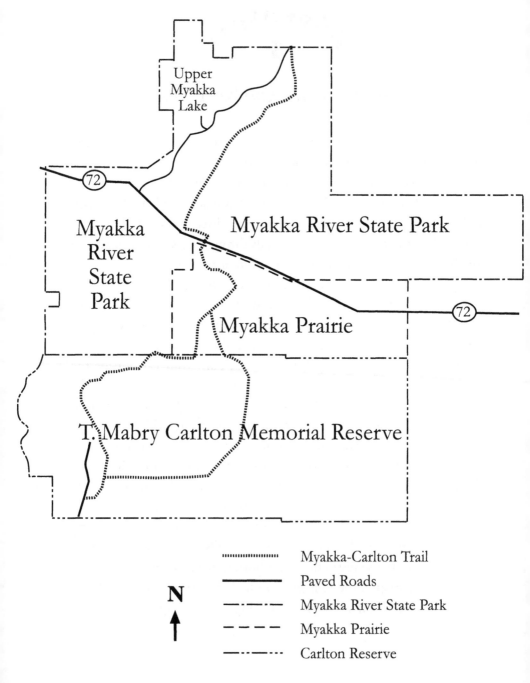

Upper Myakka Lake

72

Myakka River State Park

Myakka River State Park

Myakka Prairie

72

T. Mabry Carlton Memorial Reserve

N
↑

| | |
|---|---|
| •••••••••••• | Myakka-Carlton Trail |
| ——————— | Paved Roads |
| —·—·—·— | Myakka River State Park |
| — — — — | Myakka Prairie |
| —··—··—··— | Carlton Reserve |

## Adventure 2

# Old Miakka

This small community harbors a handful of interesting and unusual features that include a couple of Indian mounds, the region's oldest church, a century-old graveyard, a one-room schoolhouse, a picturesque view of the Myakka River, the Crowley Museum and Nature Center, and a tropical nursery of rainforest plants.

Old Miakka lies between the north boundary of the park and S.R. 70. The community was simply "Miakka" before the establishment of Myakka City on S.R. 70. When distinguishing between Miakka and Myakka City became confusing, Miakka picked up the "Old." Descendents of the area's first settlers stubbornly claimed that theirs was the proper spelling of the name and that those who spell it with a Y are incorrect.

Until recently, Old Miakka was populated primarily by people engaged in cattle ranching and other agricultural pursuits, but in recent years it has become a popular place for five- and ten-acre ranchettes whose occupants commute to work in Sarasota or Bradenton.

One of the best ways to explore Old Miakka is by bicycle. To get there, just turn left as you exit the park's north gate.

### Indian Mounds

You can see a Calusa kitchen midden (mound) at the Crowley Museum and Nature Center beside the old pioneer cabin. (Check out the next adventure for more details.) The Old Miakka Methodist Church was built on top of an Indian burial mound. I was skeptical

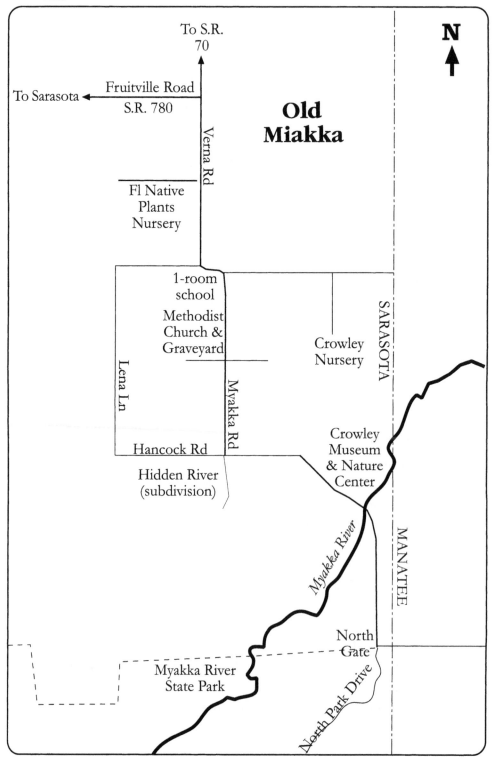

when Anna Carlton first told me about the mound.

"How do you know it's a real Indian mound?" I asked.

She carefully considered the best proof to offer. "Well, one Halloween eve the young people in the neighborhood got into some mischief over in the church yard, and the next morning it seemed there was an Indian skull on nearly every fence post in Miakka."

Later I came across another reference that reinforced the validity of local legends. In 1993, George Luer published an article in *The Florida Anthropologist* about a collector of early American Indian artifacts who purchased a pottery vessel somewhere in the northern United States because of its resemblance to Florida pottery. Upon investigation, the neck of the bottle was found to contain a yellowed piece of paper with the following inscription:

H. L. Schoff Archaeological Coll.- No. 112
Object: pottery water bottle
Location: Old myakka city Sarasota Co. Florida
Wilson Mound
Acquired: 1/12/34
Remarks: Found over a skeleton near center of mound.

Where was the Wilson mound? According to notes kept by ancestors of long-time Miakka residents, "Back in the early 1880s Mr. Wilson agreed with Mr. Bill Rawls to give an acre in the corner of his homestead for a church if Mr. Rawls would give an acre adjoining out of his homestead for a cemetery."

## Old Miakka Methodist Church

Built in 1886 by Miakka residents, this church is the oldest in Sarasota County. On the south side of the church is an old pioneer graveyard whose tombstones tell the story of the sorrows and struggles of the first settlers of the area. Church services are still held every Sunday morning in the charming little building.

### One-room Schoolhouse

This 1913-vintage wooden building sits on one corner of the S curve where Verna Road becomes Myakka Road and Wilson Road juts off to the west. It comes complete with old-fashioned desks with built-in inkwells. Some time after classes were discontinued, the building was deeded to the Myakka Community Association, a group of local residents who are restoring the building's exterior. Community Club meetings, yard sales, Christmas parties, and other local events are routinely held in the schoolhouse.

### Myakka River Bridge

The bridge is about a mile north of the park's north entrance. It was a favorite weekend hot spot for local fishermen, who would gather to socialize as they dangled lines in the Myakka River until the county posted "No Fishing" signs on each end of the little bridge. You can still get a spectacular view of the river from the bridge, and there is no better place to watch all the wading birds, ducks, and shorebirds stream in to roost late in the afternoon. I have seen thousands of birds covering the willows on the north side of the river early in the morning and near dusk. The birds seem to change their roosting destination as water levels fluctuate. Even if they are not currently roosting at the bridge, large flocks pass over it as they follow the river corridor. In the summer, the large marsh full of giant hibiscus is impressive in the early morning hours, when thousands of ten-inch, pink blossoms are in bloom.

### Crowley Tropical Fruits

This unique nursery is one of my favorite places to spend a Sunday afternoon discovering unusual tropical fruits, winding through a forest of bamboo, identifying butterflies and the plants they favor, and conversing with a pair of raucous geese. Where else can you see fifty varieties of bamboo, a remarkable collection of gingers, mangos, lychees, macadamia nuts, Chinese cinnamon, guavas, chocolate pudding trees, and fifty kinds of passion vine! The most difficult challenge is choosing which plant to take home with me at the end of my visit. Thanks to the Crowleys I have raspberries, guavas, lemons, oranges, grapefruit, bananas, avocados, carambolas, and loquats growing in my yard. I also find it interesting that nursery-owner Charlie Crowley is a descendant of one of Miakka's original pioneer families.

To get there, go to the S-curve past the Old Methodist Church and follow the signs down the dirt road for about a mile. The nursery is open from 9 until 5, seven days a week, excluding holidays.

## Florida Native Plants Nursery

Another nursery of interest to plant enthusiasts is located on Verna Road about a half-mile south of Fruitville. Even if you aren't in the market for the hardiest plants to landscape a Florida yard, it is an excellent place to learn to identify many of the plants you'll find growing in the natural areas of the Myakka Island. It's also a great place to see butterflies. Take a butterfly field guide to identify butterflies as you learn the names of the wildflowers. The owners have even planted a butterfly garden and a hummingbird garden as examples for those who may want to attract the colorful creatures to their own backyards.

# Adventure 3

## Crowley Museum and Nature Center

Over the decades, Jasper Crowley watched each new generation of increasingly urban youths grow up deprived of their pioneer heritage. As a teacher in the Sarasota County school system, he had ample opportunity to ponder the causes for the number of troubled youths and the increase in juvenile delinquency. He believed a remedy could be found by helping children and teens discover their cultural heritage and reestablish a bond with the land.

Jasper grew up on a chunk of land along the Myakka River homesteaded by his grandfather, John Crowley, just after the Civil War. He and his brothers acquired an understanding of and appreciation for their natural world as they farmed the land, crafted tools in their blacksmith shop, got to know the inhabitants of the pineywoods, and listened to stories about the Indians their grandfather encountered when the land was wilderness.

Jasper's own education was hard won, according to an Old Miakka resident who still cherishes the stories she heard from Jasper as a child. According to Shannon Blount, once Jasper reached the seventh grade he had quite a trip to make in order to continue his schooling. His parents drove him to the Verna train stop, where he boarded the train for Manatee. From there he took a boat to St. Petersburg, where he boarded another train to transport him to the high school in Clearwater.

After Jasper graduated from the University of Florida, he began teaching at the one-room schoolhouse in Miakka with a salary of $70 a month. Ms. Blount related how Jasper established the county's first hot lunch program. He would ask the students to bring vegetables to

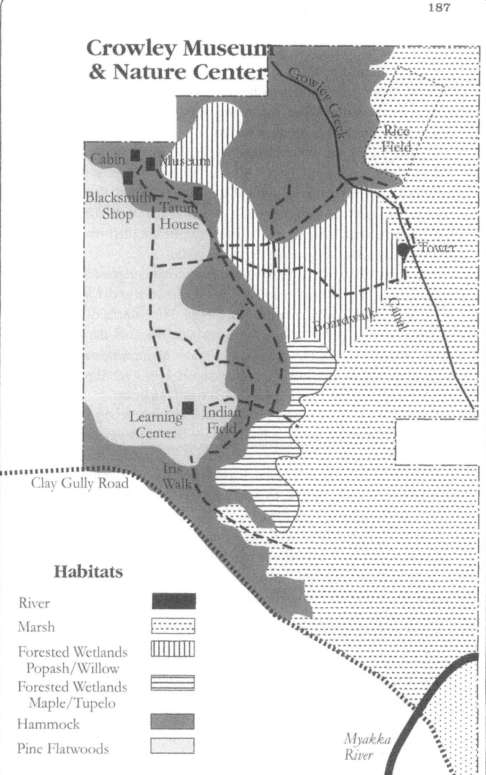

# Crowley Museum & Nature Center

Crowler Creek

Rice Field

Cabin

Museum

Blacksmith Shop

Tatum House

Tower

Boardwalk

Canal

Learning Center

Indian Field

Iris Walk

Clay Gully Road

Myakka River

## Habitats

River

Marsh

Forested Wetlands Popash/Willow

Forested Wetlands Maple/Tupelo

Hammock

Pine Flatwoods

add to meat he furnished. He simmered it all in a large pot on the wood stove in the middle of the schoolroom. As the meal cooked, the children—who would otherwise be eating cold biscuits and syrup for lunch—were often so distracted by the tantalizing aroma they could hardly keep their minds on their lessons.

Perhaps Jasper is best remembered for the many young lives he redeemed by taking in boys no one wanted—poverty-stricken, orphaned, or troubled teens, some direct from a jail cell. On Jasper's farm they learned the skills necessary to live off the land. They raised their own vegetables, butchered animals to provide their own meat, and ground sugarcane to make sugar and syrup.

Assisted by friends and neighbors, Jasper built a replica of a pioneer cabin in his backyard with the timbers hewn from yellow pine salvaged from Miakka's original dwellings. He furnished it with antiques from his grandfather's home, antiques that told the story of life in pioneer Florida. His collection of tools and implements, many of them crafted in his grandfather's blacksmith shop, were displayed in an old wooden barn, the antecedent of a small museum.

For years, Jasper Crowley invited entire classrooms of youngsters to spend a day on his working farm and see how early pioneers lived. Children learned to milk a cow; pet a docile bull; gather freshly laid eggs; feed sheep, pigs, rabbits, and turkeys; and even care for a beehive. He wanted his visitors to gain a better understanding of man's vital interdependence with nature.

When Jasper died in 1976, he left instructions that his home and land were to be used to continue to teach children about their natural and cultural heritage. His dream lives on. Each year hundreds of school children tour the cabin and museum and explore the woods that Jasper left for them.

Adults are just as enchanted by the little museum and nature center. They arrive daily and pay a small fee to step back in time and learn of Florida's past. Visitors can walk along a shaded nature trail that winds through the pinewoods, past the old Indian field, along the river marsh, out onto a boardwalk that once traversed a luxurious freshwater swamp, and up a tower overlooking the Myakka River.

Two of Sarasota County's oldest buildings have also found a home at the nature center. The Tatum House and Tatum Ridge schoolhouse were moved out to the property and restored by volunteers. You'll find them near a real sugarcane field and a functioning cane mill, which was also restored by volunteers. Next to the pioneer cabin is also a kitchen midden that was once the subject of a small archeological study conducted in the 1990s.

The nature center's days and hours of operation have fluctuated over the years, with changes in curators, staffing, and funding, but the phone number has remained the same. Call 322-1000 for the center's schedule before you make the trip. Interesting classes and special events are also scheduled throughout the year, so be sure to inquire what's on the agenda. There's no better place to experience Myakka's Cracker heritage.

To get to the Crowley Museum and Nature Center from the park on weekends and holidays, head north from the park entrance (straight ahead), over the Myakka River Bridge, and around a couple of curves. Entrance: North 27° 18' 20.6   West 82° 15' 37.4 The entrance to the nature center will be on your right a little over a mile from the park's north gate. From I-75, take S.R. 780 (Fruitville Road) east to the end of the road. Turn right onto Verna Road and follow the road for two and a half miles. The entrance to the nature center will be on your left. If you reach the Myakka River Bridge you have gone too far.

Note: Read about Jasper's brother Allen, one of the park's first superintendents, in Chapter 7.

# Adventure 4

## T. Mabry Carlton Memorial Reserve

This 24,565-acre county reserve lies along the southern boundary of Myakka River State Park, bordering about four and a half miles of the east bank of the lower Myakka River. Though you can reach it via hiking and bicycling trails from the state park, it is far easier to drive to its southern entrance. (See directions at the end of this adventure.)

The area is divided into two parts: a two-hundred-acre public-use area (with picnic tables, pavilion, restrooms, and short trails) and the large wilderness area. The public-use area features three nature trails through representative habitats of the reserve. The Blue Trail is three quarters of a mile long; the Yellow Trail is one half mile long and winds around a swamp; and the Purple Trail is a quarter mile long. As in other parts of the Myakka Island, you'll find great variance between wet and dry conditions. Summers are hot and flooded with a preponderance of mosquitoes.

There is no admission fee. Bicycles are permitted on all of the many miles of trails. Pets are not. The trail system has numbered marker posts throughout the site, but some trail markers have been added to the system since the Wild & Scenic Trails Map was published. There is a system of horse trails within the reserve for people who bring their own horses, but you must have submitted a proof of negative coggins test before riding the trails. Contact the public use area of the park at (941) 861-5000 for current reserve hours.

This piece of land has an interesting history. Besides containing an old turpentine camp, it was once part of a much larger tract owned by legendary circus owner John Ringling. I've heard he used the land for hunting, in order to feed the circus's meat-eaters, and for growing crops, to feed the herbivores. The land stayed in Ringling's estate for another two decades after he passed away, and during that time Albert Blackburn had the cattle lease. Blackburn was Mrs. Potter Palmer's ranch foreman and helped her make history with her innovative cattle-ranching techniques in Florida.

When I learned about the cattle lease from Sarasota County Parks Director John McCarthy, it solved a mystery I had pondered for years. Prairies and flatwoods in the Ringling tract were in near-pristine condition when the land was sold to the county in the 1980s. How had it been managed so well through all the years that nearby pieces of land suffered from fire exclusion? Originally, I had thought the credit went entirely to Buck Mann. When I worked for the Division of Forestry in the 1970s, he had the cattle lease on what we called the Ringling-MacArthur tract. Buck was infamous for his burning practices: he burned hundreds—sometimes thousands—of acres a day, all set to burn with the wind. In those days, foresters believed the best way to apply fire was to set a slow, backing fire (against the wind) during the winter season. Now we realize that the most natural fires move with the wind during the growing season, just like a lightning fire.

Recently I had the opportunity to interview this retired cattleman and talk about the burn strategies he learned from his father and other older Cracker cowmen. Every year he went out with a box of kitchen matches and drove down the old, two-trail dirt roads in his jeep until he saw an area that needed to burn. As he drove he would strike and throw matches, allowing the fire to burn wherever the wind carried it. It would burn until it reached a wet swamp, marsh, or hammock. Sometimes the fire burned for days.

Buck paid no attention to the location of cattle. They just moved to a hammock or wet area during a burn, just as the native animals instinctively did. There were no control lines or burn plans. If the fire passed a fence line, it just burned on neighboring land until it reached a barrier or was rained out. During dry years it burned all the way to Myakka River. In those days, there were very few residences in the area. People knew better than to build in the middle of a pine forest and allow palmettos and other shrubs to grow tall near their houses.

I was not at all surprised to discover the firing tactics that had made this eighty-year-old gentleman a celebrity in my mind. It was the land he had managed that had set the standards for Myakka River State Park's restoration goals. What did surprise me was that he had only taken over the cattle lease in the late 1960s. Who had managed it so well before that? Buck didn't know.

All the pieces fell into place when I learned about the long-time Blackburn lease. Albert would have used the same burning methods employed by Buck, applying fire as often as his cattle needed. Perhaps nature took over between the two leases. We have always noticed a higher incidence of lightning fires on the land south of the park's border than within the park. Perhaps some weather anomaly causes a greater concentration of strikes there than in other areas.

In the 1950s most of the Ringling tract was sold to the MacArthur Foundation. It remained intact until sixteen thousand acres were purchased for conservation in the 1980s. The remainder of the tract was purchased in the early 1990s, and after a land swap, the boundary lines were drawn between the Carlton Reserve and the Myakka Prairie. Sarasota County was not accustomed to managing native habitat, so when Buck Mann removed his cattle, there went the application of frequent fire. Grassy palmetto prairies grew high and thick, and pine seedlings colonized densely, unthinned by fire. By the time fire was applied, it was extremely difficult to control. The Carlton Reserve is infamous for a couple of wildfires that raged uncontrolled for days. In an unsuccessful effort to halt the spread of flames before they reached new homes that had been plunked in the middle of long-unburned pinelands, forestry plows wreaked havoc on the once-pristine uplands.

The prime lesson everyone learned from the Ringling-MacArthur land is how little time it takes for neglect to take its toll on south Florida ecosystems. I had always assumed it took half a century for Myakka River State Park to degrade to the condition it was in when I first saw it. Now we realize it happens in only a couple of decades or so.

The preserve's land managers now apply fire more frequently, though it will take more intensive management and better funding to restore it to the condition it was in when Albert and Buck left it. Meanwhile, it is still an interesting place to explore, with some of the best wetlands in Florida. Take a lunch and a pair of binoculars and walk the short trail in the recreation area. During the drier times of the year, you can take a map and compass and meander from hammock to wetland to swamp, checking out the epiphytes, bird life, and a large variety of other critters. The county park has an excellent bird checklist to get you started.

Be forewarned that this is a very large wilderness area with lots of chaotic firelines. Don't assume that a wide dirt road will lead you anywhere you want to go. It may just be an old, disked fireline that was installed randomly in front of an advancing wildfire. Don't get lost. If you are not experienced in navigating through wilderness areas, spend some time practicing at the state park, which is broken up by S.R. 72, Park Drive, and the power line, and is therefore easier to navigate.

The Carlton Reserve is located at 1800 Mabry Carlton Parkway in Venice. T. Mabry Carlton Memorial Reserve North 27°07'36.2 West 82°20'22.6 It's open daily from sunrise to 5:30 P.M. Pets, hunting, and motorized vehicles are not permitted on trails. Take I-75 to Exit 193 (Jacaranda Boulevard, old Exit 35) and go east to Border Road. Turn right and go about two and a half miles to Mabry Carlton Parkway. Turn left and follow the signs to the reserve. Call (941) 486-2547 or (941) 316-1172 if you have questions or need additional information.

# Myakka Wild & Scenic Trails Map

The key to exploring the Myakka Island comes in a two-sided, 32-inch by 27-inch color aerial map. It depicts the conservation lands in public and private ownership within the lower two-thirds of the Myakka River watershed. You can pick up a map at the preserves described in this book or at the Ranger Station at the park. A two-dollar donation is requested, though not required, to assist with printing subsequent versions of the map.

The map includes basic information such as hours of operation, acreages, phone numbers, and GPS points for preserve entrances; and illustrates trails, boat ramps and mile markers along the river.

The conservation lands described in this book are all included on the map. Listed below are properties in the Myakka Island now open to the public that were not accessible when this book was first published.

### Koch Parcel (213 acres)

(941) 851-5000; www.scgov.net. 2800 North River Road in Venice.
North gate walk-through: N 27° 06' 22.0   W 82° 20' 46.2
South gate walk-through: N 27° 06' 00.3   W 82° 20' 37.8
This site, owned and managed by Sarasota County, has primitive unmarked trails and no parking, facilities, or drinking water.

### Myakkahatchee Creek Park (160 acres)

(941) 486-2547; www.scgov.net
Park entrance: N 27° 07' 13.4   W 82° 11' 48.8
The park borders both sides of the creek and consists mostly of shady oak hammock. It features birding, canoeing, hiking and bicycling. It is owned by the City of North Port and managed by Sarasota County Parks and Recreation.

### Myakka State Forest (8,600 acres)

(941) 255-7653; River Rd entrance: N 26° 59' 25.9   W 82° 18' 12.4
The forest is open during daylight hours only, except for registered campers. Drinking water is not available in the forest. Trails are often flooded in summer and may be closed for prescribed burns any time of year. Trail closures are posted at trailheads. Hunting occurs in November and December. Pets must be on leash at all times.

## Charlotte Harbor Preserve State Park (33,518 acres)
(941) 575-5861; www.FloridaStateParks.org/CharlotteHarbor
The preserve stretches along more than 90 miles of Charlotte Harbor's shoreline and falls within both the Myakka River and Peace River watersheds. Only the portion within the Myakka River watershed is depicted. Mangrove forests and salt marshes comprise the majority of the preserve, but public access areas have been established at upland points. Most of the land is remote and primitive wilderness.

## Deer Prairie Creek Preserve (10,128 acres) (941) 861-5000
A parking lot for both cars and horse trailers is located off US 41, west of I-75 on the north side of the road. There are no restrooms or water available.

This property is part of a joint acquisition between SWFWMD and Sarasota County to protect the floodplain of the river and the water quality of the water sources within the region. Sarasota County manages all lands in Deer Prairie Creek for public use and recreation activities. The site includes pine flatwoods, hammock, depression marshes, dry prairie and scrub. There are two equestrian loop trails and access to over 60 miles of hiking trails. The preserve was not open to the public when the map was produced, so trails are not depicted on the first edition of the map. You can use a search tool on the County and SWFWMD websites to locate trail maps: www.swfwmd.state.fl.us and www.scgov.net.

## Sleeping Turtles (200 acres) (941) 861-5000; www.scgov.net
The park entrance at 3462 Border Road.
This park has about five miles of walking trails, a canoe landing but no boat launch, and no facilities.

## Rocky Ford (1,391 acres) (941) 861-5000; www.scgov.net
This preserve on the west side of the Myakka River has three miles of river frontage. The site is mostly pine flatwoods, mesic hammocks, and depression wetlands. Bald eagles, wood storks, and various wading birds inhabit this area. Florida panther have been documented on this site. This site is contiguous with the county's Pinelands Reserve on the west side of the river, Myakka River State Park on the north and east, and the County's T. Mabry Carlton Jr. Memorial Reserve on the southeast.

# Adventure 5

## The Jelks Preserve

Paddling down the lower Myakka River a mile or so past Snook Haven, you'll pass through about a mile and a half of the kind of wild beauty that won the river its "Wild and Scenic" designation: a canopy of oaks reaching for the opposite shore; marshy banks lush with ferns and swamp lilies; palms straight and tall or reclining from high embankments. Like each of the other pieces of the Myakka Island, this area has its own story of preservation and its own hero, or, in this case, heroine.

Of course, there are many people who play a role in the acquisition or protection of each piece of property. But in each case there is usually one person who had the vision, who motivated others, and who persevered against adversity. For the state park, perhaps it was Arthur Edwards. For the Oscar Scherer State Park addition, Jon Thaxton led the crusade. Mabry Carlton was most instrumental in acquisition of the Carlton Reserve (which is why it was named for him after his death). For the Jelks Preserve (and perhaps the river itself), it was Mary Jelks.

Those who admire her call her Dr. Mary. She certainly isn't the kind of benefactor you imagine when you hear of philanthropic purchases of conservation land. I picture a sympathetic, wealthy socialite or land baron, perhaps motivated as much by tax advantage as by charity. Mary lives in an unremarkable house in an older section of town. She drives a pickup truck that is probably old enough to qualify for a special license plate. She reuses everything she has already recycled at least twice and spends her time, now that she and her husband have retired from medical practice, fighting for what she thinks is most important. Florida's citizens, visitors, and future residents should consider themselves lucky that she puts a high priority on the fate of the Myakka River.

Dr. Mary is the stuff legends are made of. I can imagine myself at age 102, answering the questions of some young park ranger: "Yes, I knew Dr. Mary. It's all true, what they say. She could outwork half a dozen park rangers on a ninety-eight-degree summer day." Mary spent days and weeks and months and years going to meetings, writing letters, and fighting for legislation to protect the river. And I am sure she has personally hauled out at least a ton and a half of garbage on river cleanups over the years. I can also attest that she can identify even the tiniest, insignificant weed growing on a road shoulder.

As president of Friends of the Myakka River, she has already left a legacy of park improvements—a canopy walkway and tower, a stately park entrance, and restoration of acres and acres of Florida dry prairie. That's just the beginning because I am willing to bet there will be many more deeds to note before she has planted her last blazing star or pine lily in the park median.

Mary is quick to point out that it was not she alone who donated the money for the Jelks Preserve but her family, a family raised and inspired by a modest, caring matriarch. And that it was Sarasota County (with prompting from the renowned Dr. Mary) that came up with the additional funds necessary to purchase land on the brink of being sold to a land developer. She begged county land managers not to use her name when referring to the six-hundred-acre purchase. I'm glad they didn't listen to her. And I was so pleased when they acquired the land on the opposite bank, keeping at least that portion of the river always wild and scenic.

River corridors are extremely important parts of an ecosystem for conservation. Sightings and tracks (and other sign) of panther and bear have been recorded primarily along the river corridor in recent years. Much of the area's wildlife depends upon the freedom to come and go along the banks of the river without interference. And rivers that lose their ability to fluctuate with the seasons in order to accommodate human inhabitants lose their ability to function as natural systems.

You can recognize the Jelks Preserve on the lower Myakka River by the large canal that forks off to the west on the north corner of the property. By land you will find the entrance on North River Road between Venice Avenue and Center Road. You can hike a trail to the river. The property was in such need of management when it was acquired that it was difficult to explore cross-country. Now the county has been roller chopping and burning it in small sections. It will be interesting to see the progress in future years.

Most people reading this book will never canoe all the way down the Myakka River to experience its wildness where it passes through the Jelks Preserve. Jelks Preserve entrance: North 27° 05' 27.7 West 82° 20' 17.5 Very few will seek the gate on River Road to explore the scrub and wade through the muck where a stream flows into a tiny swamp. But even if you never see the egret perched on an oak branch hanging over the river, you can know that because of Dr. Mary it will always be there.

**Snowy egret**

# 10

# Two Centuries

*"We abuse the land because we regard it as a commodity belonging to us. When we see land as a community to which we belong, we may begin to use it with love and respect."*
Aldo Leopold

A war was declared that raged throughout the better part of a century. At first the adversaries were obvious—man against nature. We set out to tame our wildest rivers, drain the vast Everglades, annihilate earth's predators, straighten meandering rivers, fill our wetlands, and cover our prairies with trees as we clear-cut centuries-old forests. We suppressed fires ignited by lightning, indiscriminately exterminated insects, and moved plants and animals across continents, disrupting a precise system of checks and balances that had been perfected over thousands of years. In our arrogance, we believed that technology was wiser and more powerful than nature, and thus we set out to improve our natural world.

As the war raged across our country, Myakka became one of its historic battlegrounds. Ditches were dug and melaleuca trees were planted through wetlands in an effort to drain the marshlands and rid the land of mosquitoes. Miles and miles of firelines were installed as park rangers stood vigilant with plow and water tanker, watching for a whiff of smoke. Rows of pine trees were planted in the prairies, and the river was seined for garfish and mudfish. Troops of men scoured the countryside for rattlesnakes, and foreign vegetation was planted along riverbanks to prevent erosion.

As the century progressed, the war raged on but the foes were not so well defined. By the 1960s, we began to realize that without fire entire species of plants and animals would perish. The amazing science of fire ecology emerged. By the 1980s, we were cutting down planted pines to reclaim our prairies and plugging ditches to restore wetlands. Nature was no longer the enemy; she was our teacher. We were like children suddenly discovering that our parents' trivial rules had purpose. Fire, flood, drought, predation, insects, disease—all had a place in nature. We began to judge in terms of natural and unnatural instead of good and bad. We were still fighting the war, but which side were we on and who was the enemy?

You would think that with enlightenment would come peace. But as this twenty-first century progresses, we are no closer to peace than we were two decades ago. We win battles, only to discover more that need to be fought. Just when it seems that we Floridians understand the necessity of fire in our natural areas, a whole new set of residents moves in and we have to start all over again. Just as we cut the last melaleuca from the park, we are besieged by a new aggressive invader like cogon grass or West Indian marshgrass. As we plug ditches and the natural cycle of flood and drought is restored to our wetlands, riverside land upstream is altered and developed, changing the amount of water that flows downstream. Change the timing and length of wet and dry seasons, and massive tree die-offs occur.

The challenges of this century may soon surpass those of the last. As rural agricultural land in the Myakka Island is transformed into homesites for our expanding urban population, remaining natural areas must be kept in optimum condition if our wildland species are to survive. Frequent fire will be imperative not only to accomplish this mission but also to ensure that homes along borders are not threatened by lightning or unexpected fires.

The influx of people along wildland borders will certainly bring new invasions of non-native plants and animals to threaten our native species. If you take a trip to Lee County, you will see how melaleuca has displaced beautifully diverse pinelands. Go out and count the species of frogs at any residence in Sarasota or Manatee County. If there is only one, it's the Cuban treefrog, an invader devouring and displacing native treefrogs. Drive along our coastline and observe miles-long stretches of nothing but Brazilian pepper and you will understand the enormous threat exotic invaders are to our wildlands.

The future of Myakka depends on two factors: the energy and perseverance of those charged with managing its pieces, and the will of the people. Land management is no longer viewed as passive protection—you can't just build a fence around a natural area and expect it to prosper. Success depends on unrelenting diligence year after year. A decade of neglect could require half a century of restoration. We still don't know how to rid the watershed of West Indian marshgrass, a rare, exotic grass that took over Myakka's floodplain marshes in only six years. Three to five years of fire exclusion makes prairie uninhabitable to grasshopper sparrows. All of the individuals and organizations that care for the land that is Myakka must work together to manage it as a whole. If one manager is remiss in his or her duty, the entire ecosystem will suffer.

When I was a young park ranger, I was inspired by the noble goal of preserving a piece of paradise for all eternity. I have since come to realize that this mission is possible only as long as the public supports it. Floridians must not only understand and support the activities necessary to manage natural areas, they must also be willing to pay for them. Land management is not cheap. Funding must be found for heavy equipment to maintain firelines and to restore prairies and wetlands; for exhibits and brochures to educate Florida's residents and visitors; and for salaries for those hired to care for the land.

So what's to become of Myakka? If it is to remain the place east of Sarasota where nature, rather than man, rules, each successive generation will have to establish its own unique bond with the land. The path to that bond has been mapped throughout the tenure of humans on earth: curiosity leads to discovery, discovery to understanding, understanding to appreciation, appreciation to affection, and affection to protection. Share a little curiosity every chance you get. ᔓ

*"When one tugs at a single thing in nature, he finds it attached to the rest of the world."*
John Muir

**Great blue heron**

# ❧ Myakka A-Z ❧

**Accommodations**
> *See* Cabins; Camping

**Airboat Tours**
> Airboat tours are offered 7 days a week year-round. Tours do not run on Thanksgiving or Christmas or during thunderstorms, high winds, or periods of extremely high water. Tours leave the boat basin promptly at 10 A.M., 11:30 A.M., and 1 P.M. from June 1 through December 15. A 2:30 P.M. tour is added from December 16 through May 31. During peak season, additional boat tours are run between regularly scheduled tours.

**Backpack Camping**
> *See* Camping, Primitive

**Bee Island**
> An island of long-leaf pines surrounded by prairie, located on Ranch House Road, about 3 miles east of Park Drive. The story goes that pioneers looking for honey in a country made up mostly of treeless prairie would head out to Bee Island, thus the origin of the name. Bee Island primitive campground is located on the western edge of the pine island in a small oak hammock (5.4 miles from the trailhead).

**Bicycles, Bicycle Trails**
> Bicycles are available for rent at the park concession. Maps can be picked up at the Ranger Station. Bicycles are permitted on paved and dirt roads. They are not permitted on the nature trail, in the Wilderness Preserve, or hiking trails.

**Birding**
> Myakka River is famous for birding opportunities. During the winter and spring, the park offers beginning birding classes and has volunteer "Bird Interpreters" that set up their scopes at the Birdwalk to help visitors identify birds. A park bird list is available at the ranger station and online at www.MyakkaRiver.org.

## Brochures

Brochures available at the Ranger Station include 25 Things to Do, Bird List, Cabins, Camping, Christmas Bird Count, Florida Dry Prairie, Florida State Parks Guide, Friends of the Myakka River, Hiking & Biking, Horse Trails, Myakka Canopy Walkway, Myakka Fact Sheet, Myakka River State Park, Plant List ($), Restoring the Myakka Island, Vertebrate List ($), Wild & Scenic River, Wild & Scenic Trails Map ($), Wilderness Preserve, and Youth/Group Camp. Brochures are also available for download from www.MyakkaRiver.org.

## Bugs

*See* Mosquitoes

## Cabins

The log cabins were built by the Civilian Conservation Corps in the 1930s. Facilities include a kitchen with stove and refrigerator, a bathroom with shower, and a large sleeping room with air conditioner and fireplace. Each cabin accommodates up to 6 people with 2 double beds and a fold-away sofa bed. Reservations can be made up to 11 months in advance. The cabins are very popular, and it is often difficult to get reservations on weekends and holidays and between December and April unless you call several months in advance. Check at the Ranger Station or the website for current fees.

## Campfires

Campfires are permitted in upright grills, ground grills, and fire circles only. Bring your own firewood (you're not allowed to collect firewood in the park), or buy some at the park concession.

## Camping, Family

Each site in Big Flats and in Old Prairie campgrounds has water, electricity, a picnic table, and a grill or fire ring. Both campgrounds have restrooms with showers. No sewer hookups, but a dump station is located close to Old Prairie Camp. Sites accommodate tents, vans, and trailers or motor homes up to 35 feet long. There are no buffers between most of the sites, which can make for crowded conditions in season (December through April) and holidays. Reservations are highly recommended and can be made up to 11 months in advance. There are plans for a new campground across the road from Old Prairie Campground.

## Camping, Group

Large sites for organized groups, such as Scouts and church groups, are available for tent camping only. Each site has a large shaded area to set up tents, a fire circle, a cooking area, a hose bib, and picnic tables. One small restroom with showers services the 3 campsites.

## Camping, Primitive

Six campgrounds are located along the 39-mile hiking trail. Each campground has 3 campsites, each of which can accommodate up to 4 people. Two campsites can be reserved; the third is available on a first-come basis.

## Concession

Myakka Outpost rents bicycles and canoes and sells snacks, sandwiches, gator stew, a few grocery items, camping supplies, souvenirs, nature books and field guides, T-shirts, and gifts. The elevated building constructed in 2008 provides a view of the Upper Lake and an expanded menu from the previous concession. It is open from 9 A.M. until 5 P.M. 7 days a week from December through May. Reduced days and hours apply from June through November. Check at the Ranger Station for the current schedule. To reach Myakka Outpost, call 941-923-1120.

## Canoes

Bring your own or rent from the park concession. For current fees, check at the Ranger Station, concession, or web page.

## Dogs

*See* Pets

## Elevation

The elevation of Myakka River State Park ranges from 14 to 45 feet above sea level.

## Facilities

Myakka River State Park contains several picnic areas (including four pavilions), Visitor Center, a park concession with a small restaurant, 2 campgrounds with a total of 76 sites, 5 log cabins, a group camp with 3 sites, 39 miles of hiking trails, 6 primitive camp areas, 15.5 miles of horse trails, a .6 mile nature trail, a canopy walkway with a 74-foot tower, a 7-mile scenic drive, small art gallery in the ranger station, fishing pier, boat ramp, restrooms, and a boardwalk on the Upper Lake.

## Fees, Entrance

Park entrance fees are nominal. A detailed fee schedule is available at the Ranger Station and online at www.FloridaStateParks.org/MyakkaRiver.

## Fishing

A Florida fishing license is required for anyone 15 years old and older. Florida residents at least 65 years of age can obtain a free lifetime fishing permit from the Florida Fish and Wildlife Conservation Commission. Those who fish within the park must obey Florida fishing laws, such as those regarding size limits and bag limits. Anglers fish for black bass (large-mouth bass), catfish, bluegill, and other panfish. A wheelchair-accessible fishing pier and a fish identification exhibit is located near the weir at Upper Myakka Lake.

## Friends of the Myakka River

This is a nonprofit group established to protect, preserve, and support Myakka River State Park and the Florida Wild and Scenic Myakka River. The group raises funds and provides volunteer services to increase the enjoyment of visitors to the park and river. Membership fees are low; members receive 4 newsletters and 12 days of free entrance to the park each year.

## Frog Calls

*The Calls of Frogs and Toads* by Lang Elliott is available from Naturesound Studio (www.northsoundmusic.com).

## Hiking Trail

The 39-mile trail was built and is maintained by the Florida Trail Association. Trail maps are available at the Ranger Station.

## History, Encapsulated

Prior to 1850, the Myakka River was labeled "Asternal River" on English maps. A Seminole Indian reportedly told a surveyor in the 1850s that the name of the river was "Myakka," though no similar-sounding word exists in either of the Seminole languages. Between the

1850s and 1930s, cattle grazed on open prairie. The first acquisition of land for the park occurred in 1934—a purchase of 17,070 acres from the Palmer estate and a donation of 1,920 acres in the memory of Bertha Honore Palmer. Between 1934 and 1941, the Civilian Conservation Corps constructed facilities, cleared firelines, and developed the park. Myakka River was formally dedicated in 1941 and officially opened to the public in 1942.

## Honore Campground

This primitive campground is accessible only to hikers and is 8.5 miles from the trailhead. It is an extension of the southern Bee Island trail loop and offers similar diversity. Honore was named by the Florida Trail Association, which built the trail and campgrounds, after the maiden name of Bertha Palmer of Chicago, who once owned much of the land that is now the park. The site is a dense hammock of cabbage palms and live oaks and makes a perfect wilderness retreat.

## Horse Trails

Bring your own horse and register to ride the 15.5-mile, multi-looped trail. Proof of a negative Coggins test is required. There's an additional fee for use of the horse trail. The trail passes through hammock, prairie, and wetlands and is extremely wet and buggy during the summer.

## Hours of Operation

The park is open from 8 A.M. until sunset 7 days a week (including holidays).

## Kayaks

Bring your own or rent from the concession. For current fees, check at the Ranger Station, concession, or website.

## Location

The park is located in Sarasota 9 miles east of I-75 on S.R. 72. Take I-75 to Exit 205 (Clark Road).

## Mosquitoes

Mosquitoes peak at the height of the rainy season (usually September). They can be pesky any time of the year about a half-hour after sunset and a half-hour before sunrise.

## Mossy Hammock Camp

The closest primitive campground to North Drive is a 2.2-mile shady hike. The site is located in densely shaded hammock. Also accessible by bicycle.

## Myakka Friends Gallery & Gifts

Friends of Myakka River sponsors a small art gallery and gift shop at the Ranger Station near the State Road 72 park entrance. Proceeds are used to support land management and education projects at the park and on the river.

## Myakka Movies

Five videos in the Visitor Center provide information about the park.

## Myakka Wild and Scenic Trails Map

The large 2-sided color aerial photos depict the public and conservation lands along the Myakka Wild & Scenic River, with roads, hiking trails, and other facilities on each tract.

## Nature Walks

Ranger-guided walks are often scheduled during the winter and spring. Check at the Ranger Station for the current schedule

## Oak Grove Campground

This primitive campground is accessible by hiking or biking. The trail spurs off the northern Bee Island loop and traverses open prairie most of the way, though the last mile of the 10-mile route follows the edge of Deer Prairie Slough. Maples, oaks, elms, and bays make up the canopy of the slough, and the groundcover consists of ferns and lush, green subtropical plant life.

## Panther Point Campground

This primitive campground is accessible only to hikers and is about 4.5 miles east of Honore (13 miles from the trailhead). Upon leaving Honore, the trail enters open prairie for most of the route, skirting a few small bayheads and isolated tree islands. The densely shaded location was chosen for its feeling of cozy isolation.

## Pavilions

Four covered pavilions are available for rent, with reservations accepted up to a year in advance. Reserved signs are posted on pavilions that have been rented for the day. Pavilions that have not been reserved are available free on a first-come basis.

## Permits, Family and Individual

Annual entrance permits, which can be purchased at any state park, allow free entry for day use for all state parks except Homosassa Springs Wildlife Park and the Skyway Fishing Pier. These permits allow 24-hour use of most Florida state parks as well as free entrance for horse trails and diving facilities.

## Pets

Pets are permitted on a 6-foot hand-held leash. They are not permitted in cabins or other buildings, in the Wilderness Preserve, on tours, or in concession-owned canoes. Pets should not be taken to areas where alligators may be encountered.

## Prairie Campground

The most remote primitive campground is 14.1 miles from the trailhead. It is in a small pine island in the midst of a large, open prairie. Be careful with campfires as the surrounding habitat is fire dependent, thus quite flammable.

## Ranger Programs

Program schedules are posted at the Ranger Station and at campgrounds. Programs include campfire programs, birding classes, and nature walks. Special programs can be scheduled for groups when rangers are available.

## Reservations

Call Reserve America at 800-326-3521 to make reservations for family camping, cabins, or pavilions. Call the park Ranger Station at 941-361-6511 to reserve primitive or group campsites.

## Size

The park is located in Sarasota and Manatee Counties and contains 37,198 acres (58 square miles), which includes Myakka Prairie, an 8,249-acre tract titled to Southwest Florida Water Management District.

## Telephone Numbers

Ranger Station: 941-361-6511
Park concession: 941-923-1120
Myakka Wildlife Tours: 941-377-5797
There are 2 public phones in the park, 1 at the Ranger Station and 1 at the concession.

## Tours

*See* Airboat Tours; Tram Tours; Ranger Programs

## Trails

*See* Bicycling, Bicycle Trails; Hiking Trail; Horse Trails

## Tram Tours

Myakka Wildlife Tours' Tram Safari runs December 16 through May 31. Regular scheduled times are 1:00 and 2:30 P.M and during peak season an 11:30 A.M tour is added. Tram riders receive a discount ticket for an airboat ride.

## Visitor Center

Maps, brochures, displays, and Myakka Movies are located in the old horse barn across from the Ranger Station. The building was formerly the old museum and the interpretive center.

## Website

www.MyakkaRiver.org and www.FloridaStateParks.org/MyakkaRiver

## Wilderness Preserve

The preserve encompasses 7,500 acres south of S.R. 72 that includes Lower Myakka Lake. Get a wilderness permit before entering. The area is open from 8 A.M. until sunset and is limited to 30 visitors per day. Pets, bicycles, and motorized land vehicles are not permitted.

## Youth Camp

*See* Camping, Group

# Plant List

| Common name | Latin Name |
|---|---|
| arrowhead | *Sagittaria sp* |
| aster | *Aster sp* |
| bachelor's buttons | *Polygala rugelii* |
| Bahiagrass | *Paspalum notatum* |
| bald cypress | *Taxodium distichum* |
| beardtongue | *Penstemon multiflorus* |
| black gum | *Nyssa sylvatica* |
| blazing star | *Liatris sp* |
| blueberry | *Vaccinium darrowii , V. myrsinites* |
| Brazilian pepper | *Schinus terebinthifolius* |
| broomsedge | *Andropogon virginicus,* *A. glomeratus* |
| bulrush | *Scirpus validus* |
| butterfly orchid | *Encyclia tampensis* |
| butterflyweed | *Asclepias sp* |
| buttonbush | *Cephalanthus occidentalis* |
| cabbage palm | *Sabal palmetto* |
| canna lily | *Canna flaccida* |
| cardinal airplant | *Tillandsia fasciculata* |
| Carolina ash | *Fraxinus caroliniana* |
| cherry laurel | *Prunus caroliniana* |
| citrus | *Citrus sp* |
| coffee, wild | *Psychotria nevosa, P. sulzneri* |
| cogon grass | *Imperata brasilensis* |
| cordgrass | *Spartina bakeri* |
| cypress, bald | *Taxodium distichum* |
| deer tongue | *Carphephorus paniculatus* |
| dogwood, stiff Cornel | *Cornus foemina* |
| fire flag | *Thalia geniculata* |
| firebush | *Hamelia patens* |
| Florida paintbrush | *Carphephorus corymbosus* |
| gallberry | *Ilex glabra* |
| gammagrass | *Tripsacum dactyloides* |
| giant leatherfern | *Acrostichum danaeifolium* |

| | |
|---|---|
| golden club | *Orontium aquaticum* |
| goldenaster | *Pityopsis graminifolia* |
| goldenrod | *Solidago sp* |
| hempvine | *Mikania cordifolia, M. scandens* |
| hickory, pignut | *Carya glabra* |
| hickory, water | *Carya aquatica* |
| holly, dahoon | *Ilex cassine* |
| hydrilla | *Hydrilla verticillata* |
| Indian grass (Western) | *Sorghastrum sp* |
| Indian grass | *Sorghastrum secundum* |
| laurel oak | *Quercus laurifolia* |
| lime prickly ash, wild lime | *Zanthoxylum fagara* |
| little bluestem | *Andropogon sp* |
| live oak | *Quercus virginiana* |
| lizard's tail | *Saururus cernuus* |
| loblolly bay | *Gordonia lasianthus* |
| longleaf pine | *Pinus palustris* |
| maidencane | *Panicum hemitomon* |
| maple, red | *Acer rubrum* |
| marlberry | *Ardisia escallonoides* |
| marsh marigold | *Bidens laevis* |
| marsh pink | *Sabatia grandiflora, S. bartramii* |
| meadow beauty | *Rhexia cubensis, R. mariana* |
| melaleuca | *Melaleuca quinquenervia* |
| mulberry | *Morus rubra* |
| myrsine | *Myrsine floridana* |
| palmetto | *Serenoa repens* |
| paragrass | *Brachiaria mutica* |
| pickerelweed | *Pontederia cordata* |
| pine lily | *Lilium catesbai* |
| pineapple airplant | *Tillandsia Utricularia* |
| pinewoods dropseed | *Sporobols junceus* |
| pop ash (Carolina ash) | *Fraxinus caroliniana* |
| rattlesnakemaster | *Eryngium yuccifolium* |
| red bay | *Persia barbonia* |
| royal fern | *Osmunda regalis* |
| runner oak | *Quercus minima, Q. pumila* |
| sabal palm | *Sabal palmetto* |
| sand cypress | *Hypericum fasciculatum* |

| | |
|---|---|
| saw palmetto | *Serenoa repens* |
| silver bay | *Magnolia virginiana* |
| slash pine | *Pinus elliottii* |
| smartweed | *Persicaria sp (Polygonum sp)* |
| St. John's-wort | *Hypericum sp* |
| sumac | *Rhus copallina* |
| sunflower | *Helianthus agresits,* |
| | *H. angustifolius* |
| swamp bay | *Persea palustrus* |
| swamp fern | *Blechnum serrulatum* |
| swamp lily | *Crinum americanum* |
| switch grass (Western) | *Panicum sp* |
| tiger lily (pine lily) | *Lilium catesbai* |
| viburnum | *Viburnum obovatum* |
| water hickory | *Carya aquatica* |
| water hyacinth | *Eichhornia crassies* |
| water paspalum | *Paspalum repens* |
| water spangle ferns | *Salvinia minima* |
| wax myrtle | *Myrica cerifera* |
| West Indian marshgrass | *Hymenachne amplexicaulis* |
| white stopper | *Eugenia axillaris* |
| white vine | *Sarcostemma clausum* |
| wild vanilla | *Carhephorus odoritissimus* |
| willow | *Salix caroliniana* |
| wiregrass | *Aristida sp* |
| witch grass | *Dichanthelium sp* |
| yellow waterlily | *Nymphaea mexicana* |
| yellow-eyed grass | *Xyris sp* |

# ✌ **Meet the Artists** ᶜᵉ

Florida native **Christy Burch** grew up the daughter of a park ranger and lived in half a dozen different state parks as a child. Now a park ranger at Myakka River, she loves to be outdoors and has a special fascination and appreciation for Florida's hepeto-fauna. Her aspiration is to be as great a naturalist and resource manager as her father. (Matanzasnine@aol.com)

Originally from McKee City, New Jersey, **Joanna Lee Miller** now lives in Sarasota. A recent Ringling School of Art and Design graduate, she is a freelance illustrator and character designer. (BadKid1066@aol.com)

**Joel Bewley** acquired his love for the land as a child, roaming the hills of Tennessee. He is currently a student at Ringling School of Art and Design.

**Harry McVay** is a Sarasota native who spent much of his childhood fishing the Myakka River, roving hammocks and flatwoods, observing critters, and studying alligators. He sold his first painting, of a *Tyrannosaurus rex,* in second grade and won a ribbon at the county fair for his butterfly collection. Harry earned degrees from the University of Florida and the Ringling School of Art and Design in the 1970s and went on to create what he knows best—images of natural Florida and its country back roads. His accurate, detailed illustrations and paintings in watercolor and acrylics depict a realistic style that has made him a favorite of many conservation agencies for inspiring appreciation of the real Florida, among them several Florida state parks, the Florida Department of Environmental Protection, and the Nature Conservancy. (mackeyart@hotmail.com)

# Index

Here are some other books from Pineapple Press on related topics. For a complete catalog, visit our website at www.pineapplepress.com. Or write to Pineapple Press, P.O. Box 3889, Sarasota, Florida 34230-3889, or call (800) 746-3275.

*Florida Magnificent Wilderness* by James Valentine and D. Bruce Means. A visual journey through some of the most precious wild areas in the state, presenting the breathtaking beauty preserved in state lands, parks, and natural areas. Valentine has used his camera to record images of the state's remote wilderness areas. Means has written the detailed captions and main text, "Florida's Rich Biodiversity."

*Exploring Wild South Florida,* Fourth Edition by Susan Jewell. The new edition includes more than 40 new natural areas and covers Broward, Collier, Miami-Dade, Hendry, Lee, Monroe, and Palm Beach Counties.

*Florida's Uplands, Volume 1: Florida's Natural Ecosystems and Native Species* by Ellie Whitney and D. Bruce Means. Taken from the earlier book *Priceless Florida,* updated, and modified for a standalone book, this volume discusses the well-drained areas of Florida, including the high pine grasslands, flatwoods and prairies, interior scrub, hardwood hammocks, rocklands and caves, and beach dunes.

*Florida's Wetlands, Volume 2: Florida's Natural Ecosystems and Native Species* by Ellie Whitney, D. Bruce Means, and Anne Rudloe. Taken from the earlier book *Priceless Florida,* updated, and modified for a standalone book, this volume focuses on interior wetlands, seepage wetlands, marshes, flowing-water swamps, beaches and marine marshes, and mangrove swamps.

*Florida's Waters, Volume 3: Florida's Natural Ecosystems and Native Species* by Ellie Whitney, D. Bruce Means, and Anne Rudloe. Taken from the earlier book *Priceless Florida,* updated, and modified for a standalone book, this volume covers the fresh- and saltwater systems of Florida, including lakes and ponds; rivers and streams; springs; aquatic caves; estuarine waters and seafloors; submarine meadows; sponge, rock, and reef communities; and the Gulf and Atlantic Ocean.

*Florida's Living Beaches* by Blair and Dawn Witherington. Comprehensive accounts of more than 800 species found on 700 miles of Florida's sandy beaches. Meticulously researched with full-color illustrations throughout.

*Nature's Steward* by Nicholas Penniman. This well-researched volume chronicles the efforts of the Conservancy of Southwest Florida, founded in 1964, to protect and preserve sensitive ecosystems during one of the greatest building booms in American history. Main topics are land acquisition, managing for growth, and water issues.

*The Everglades: River of Grass* by Marjory Stoneman Douglas. Before 1947, when Marjory Stoneman Douglas named it a "river of grass," the Everglades was considered a vast, worthless swamp. She focused the world's attention on the need to preserve this unique ecosystem, the only Everglades on earth.

*Marjory Stoneman Douglas: Voice of the River* by Marjory Stoneman Douglas. This is the story of an influential life told in a unique and spirited voice. Marjory Stoneman Douglas, nationally known as the first lady of conservation and the woman who "saved" the Everglades, was the founder of Friends of the Everglades, a feminist, a fighter for racial justice, and always a writer.

*Florida's Birds,* Second Edition by David S. Maehr and Herbert W. Kale II. Now with color throughout, this new edition includes 30 new species accounts. Sections on bird study, feeding, and habitats; threatened and endangered species; exotic species; and bird conservation.

*Snake in the Grass* by Larry Perez. The nonnative Burmese python is now known to be reproducing freely in the Florida Everglades, wreaking havoc on the delicate balance of this unique ecosystem. An Everglades naturalist describes how the story unfolding in the famed River of Grass provides new opportunities to revisit our understanding of wilderness and man's place within it.

*Florida's Rivers* by Charles Boning. An overview of Florida's waterways and detailed information on 60 of Florida's rivers, covering each from source to end. From the Blackwater River in the western Panhandle to the Ichetucknee and Kissimmee Rivers in central Florida to the Miami River in south Florida.

CPSIA information can be obtained
at www.ICGtesting.com
Printed in the USA
BVHW01s1924261117
500979BV00004B/7/P